KIDS EXPLORE AMERICA'S JEWISH HERITAGE

Westridge Young Writers Workshop

John Muir Publications
Santa Fe, New Mexico

When you read this book you will learn
All kinds of people make the world turn.
Each is different in his or her own way,
We want you to know that that's OK.
These heroes have taught us things we didn't know,
Now along with us you can grow.

John Muir Publications, P.O. Box 613, Santa Fe, NM 87504
Copyright © 1996 by Jefferson County School District N. R-1
Cover © 1996 John Muir Publications
All rights reserved.
Printed in the United States of America

First edition. First printing September 1996.

Library of Congress Cataloging-in-Publication Data
Kids explore America's Jewish heritage / Westridge Young
    Writers Workshop. — 1st ed.
    p.   cm.
    Summary: Presents writings by students in grades three to seven on topics of Jewish culture,
including sports, food, history, and art.
    ISBN 1-56261-274-3 (pbk.)
    1. Jews—United States—History—Juvenile literature. 2. Children's writings, American. [1.
Jews—United States. 2. Children's writings.] I. Westridge Young Writers Workshop.
E184.J5K386   1996
973'.04924—dc20   96-4773
                                                                        CIP
                                                                        AC

Editors Rob Crisell, Peggy Schaefer, Elizabeth Wolf
Production Nikki Rooker, Marie Vigil
Graphics Manager Sarah Horowitz
Design Susan Surprise
Cover Art Tony D'Agostino
Typesetting Marcie Pottern
Printer Publisher's Press

Distributed to the book trade by
Publishers Group West
Emeryville, California

CONTENTS

ACKNOWLEDGMENTS

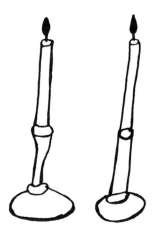

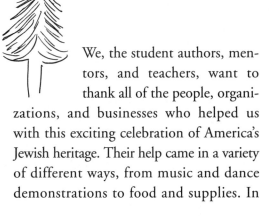

We, the student authors, mentors, and teachers, want to thank all of the people, organizations, and businesses who helped us with this exciting celebration of America's Jewish heritage. Their help came in a variety of different ways, from music and dance demonstrations to food and supplies. In the Participants section at the end of the book, we have included a list of all the people who volunteered their talents, time, or financial assistance. We hope we haven't left anyone off our list because we are grateful for all the resources provided to us by these fine folks. We couldn't have done it without them.

STUDENTS' PREFACE

Learning about a culture is always exciting, fascinating, and full of surprises. Whether you're Jewish or you just want to know more about the American Jewish culture, this book will provide plenty of answers. It might also raise plenty of questions that we can't answer in this book. To help make this book more fun to read, we have a few tips for you to follow along the way.

The most important thing to remember is that each Jewish American and his or her family is different. Jewish American ancestors came from many different countries throughout the world. When they came to America, they brought their traditions with them and passed them down to the next generation. Jewish Americans feel proud to be Americans, so they have lots of American customs and beliefs, too. Although this book deals with Jewish Americans as a group, they all believe, think, and do different things.

To make this book easier for our non-Jewish readers to understand, we would like to explain a few things. Most Jewish people follow the teachings of the Torah—the Hebrew Bible—which includes the Five Books of Moses, the Book of the Prophets, and the Book of the Writings. They also follow the Oral Laws, which are now written in many volumes of books called the Talmud. Most Jewish traditions, customs, practices, and beliefs come from these books. Most Americans would recognize the written Torah as the Old Testament in their Christian Bible.

One of the goals of our book is to teach respect and understanding. For this reason, we are respectful of the custom that many Jews have of not completely spelling out the word "G-d." Using the "G-d" spelling is considered respectful because one of the Ten Commandments says to not take the Lord's name in vain. So throughout this book, you will always see G-d's name spelled this way.

A glossary of difficult-to-pronounce words is provided toward the back of the book. Although many of the words have pronunciation keys next to them, turn to the glossary for any additional help.

A common belief among Jews is that community is extremely important. There are various Jewish organizations working to help communities all over the United States. Some of the larger and more widely known organizations are the Coalition for Alternatives in Jewish Education (CAJE), the World Zionist Organization (WZO), the Anti-Defamation League (ADL), and many Allied Jewish Federations in communities across America. These organizations do lots of things, such as raising money for synagogues and trips to Israel, providing educational programs and supplies, and fighting anti-semitism in each community. These organizations provide a lot of support for Jewish Americans and for institutions in the State of Israel. They help people who aren't Jewish, too. You'll find information about some of these groups in this book's Resource Guide.

Each community of Jews has the same basic Jewish belief in one G-d and the Torah, but Judaism is not just a religion, it's also a culture. The three main branches of Judaism include the Orthodox, Conservative, and Reform. Each of these is special in its own way. Here is a simple explanation of each of the types of Judaism. Orthodox is the most traditional, and Orthodox Jews follow more of the Torah's laws in their daily lives. Reform Jews learn the laws of the Torah and then follow only the ones they find meaningful. Conservative Jews are in the middle—they enjoy a traditional service, but they don't do all the daily rituals of the Torah.

The differences between all three branches of Judaism lie in how people choose to observe their faith. We know some people have strong feelings about their own beliefs, and we hope nobody feels bad about anything we write. Our writing is not meant to hurt any person's feelings.

We hope these tips answer a few questions that you might have while you read this book. The more you learn, the more you'll understand our great country.

TEACHERS' PREFACE

Welcome to another title in the Kids Explore series! Once again, the Westridge Young Writers Workshop in Colorado has written an interesting book for you to explore. In this book, you will learn about America's Jewish heritage and people.

The journey that produced this book began more than a year ago with a group of teachers planning and organizing an outline. We were a group of individuals, both Jewish and non-Jewish, with a common goal. We wanted to help people understand and teach the Jewish American culture.

This unique book was written by a group of 100 young authors from the Denver metropolitan area. What was special about this particular book is that we not only had Jewish and non-Jewish authors, we also had representatives from different branches of Judaism. During the summer writers' workshop, the young student authors, high school mentors, and teachers experienced the Jewish American culture through art and cooking projects, Jewish songs and dances, speakers, and most of all, through the sharing, caring, and respect they showed one another.

The teachers realized that, although the adults were important, it was the kids who would make this project successful. During the workshop, we teachers wished we had some of the kids' energy. We admired the willingness of the students to learn, and their creativity and determination to write—and then write some more.

This book was written by kids for kids, but it is still a wonderful book for teachers. The information it presents is easy to assimilate and brings out a unique perspective of the Jewish heritage. Many chapters have information that is cross-referenced to other chapters. We know this will be helpful for you when preparing lessons or expanding your own knowledge. Whether you want to find a hands-on craft, learn about a Jewish holiday, share a story, or take a look at history from a different perspective, it is all here at your fingertips.

Kids Explore America's Jewish Heritage emphasizes the importance of understanding, accepting, and respecting others. We hope that you will share this book with others, giving them a chance to learn about the Jewish American culture.

After you enjoy this book, remember to look for the other excellent titles in this series: *Kids Explore America's Hispanic Heritage, Kids Explore America's African American Heritage, Kids Explore America's Japanese American Heritage, Kids Explore the Heritage of Western Native Americans,* and *Kids Explore the Gifts of Children with Special Needs.*

The authors, teachers, and publisher welcome any comments from readers. We would like to hear how you used this book and integrated it into the experiences of your students or your family.

HISTORY

The history of our people is very long.
Through hardship and struggles we became strong.
We came to America, a beautiful land,
Here we found freedom that was more than grand.

We have divided our history chapter into three parts. We start with Jewish people in America, telling how they came to this country, what happened when they got here, and some of the important contributions they made to America. The second part tells the personal stories of two special Americans. They have been an important part of history and have helped to build a stronger America. The third part discusses the long past that Jewish immigrants brought with them to America, beginning in Biblical times. To make this part easier to follow, we take you on a walk through some exciting events in Jewish history.

The Jewish holidays all have religious significance, and they also relate to events in Jewish history. For this reason, Jewish history and the Jewish religion are very important to one another. They are parts of the same puzzle. If you try to look at them separately, the picture is incomplete. Because of this, you may want to refer to the Holidays and Festivals chapter of this book when studying this history.

Jewish history covers so much time that we couldn't give you all the details, but there are many good books on Jewish history at your local libraries. We have given you only a taste, and we hope it makes you want to learn more. When you read this history chapter, think of it as the three separate puzzle pieces of the history of Jewish Americans. When you put them together, you will know a lot about the Jewish heritage.

JEWISH PEOPLE IN AMERICA

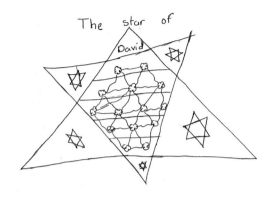

Over the years, many people have come to America for religious freedom. It is hard for us to imagine, but in many countries people are not free to worship as they wish. Sometimes the country's leader will decide which god people should worship and how they should worship him. This has gone on for thousands of years. America, however, has been different.

In the 1500s, many pilgrims came to America from Europe because they didn't want to worship the way a king or queen said they had to. In Spain, Queen Isabella persecuted the Jews because of their religious beliefs and practices. Many of them

moved to other countries to get away from this awful time known as the Spanish Inquisition. The first Jews from Spain came to America in the 1500s. When they got off the boat in New Amsterdam, the governor and some of the townspeople were worried because they thought the Jews were different. After several weeks of arguing, a letter from the company in Holland that did business in New Amsterdam said that the Jews could stay if they made themselves useful. This was wonderful news! They had a new home where they didn't have to hide who they were. Soon they became merchants, craftsmen, and farmers.

Ten years later, the British took over the rule of New Amsterdam and renamed the colony New York. The Jews were allowed to stay, but they still had to struggle to gain full rights. In 1730, the Jews were able to build their first synagogue, in New York City.

As more Jews came to America, some stayed in New York and others moved to places such as Massachusetts, Pennsylvania, Rhode Island, and South Carolina. Many Jews chose Rhode Island because of the religious freedom, important seaports, and business centers there. In 1763, they

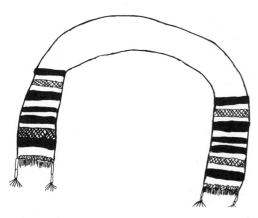

built the Touro Synagogue, in honor of the first Rhode Island rabbi, Issac Touro. By 1776, Newport, Rhode Island, had a population of 7,500, including 1,200 Jews—the largest Jewish community in America at that time. President George Washington once visited and spoke in the Touro Synagogue. Today, it is the oldest standing synagogue in the continental United States and is also a National Shrine. In 1794, the Jewish community in Charleston, South Carolina, built the second oldest synagogue in the United States.

During the American Revolution in the late 1700s, about 3,000 Jews lived in the 13 British colonies. At the end of the Revolution, each of the 13 new states had its own constitution and laws. Some states wouldn't let Jewish people vote or hold a political office. Thomas Jefferson was the governor of Virginia at that time, and he was against these laws. Virginia passed the "Statute of Religious Liberty." This gave all Virginians religious freedom and civil rights. After that, many other states did the same thing.

When the Constitution of the United States was written, the Jews hoped that it would give equal rights to all citizens. They were happy when they read the First Amendment, which said, "Congress shall make no law respecting an establishment of religion." This meant that anybody could practice any religion they wanted to. At last, Jews were given all their civil rights. Now they were citizens of a country that didn't discriminate against them because they were Jewish.

Things still weren't settled in Europe, and Europeans kept hearing about "The Golden Land"—America. Between 1820 and 1870, the population of America grew from 10 million to 40 million. Some of these new Americans were Jewish.

Jews were very active in the fight against slavery. But during the Civil War, most Jews were loyal to the area in which they lived. Jews in the South fought for the Confederacy, while Jews in the North fought for the Union Army.

During the mass immigration that lasted from the late 1880s to the early 1920s, many Jews and other immigrants came to America. The new life was hard at first. Many Jewish immigrants went to the Lower East Side of New York, where they found family and friends. Their family and friends helped them get through the first confusing months in their new country.

Most of the Jewish immigrants spoke Yiddish, which is a mixture of German and Hebrew. They soon realized they needed a source of information they could understand. Newspapers and magazines printed in Yiddish became very popular, especially in New York and Chicago, where they were published. In 1885, the first

Yiddish daily paper came out. By 1900, it had a circulation of 100,000. The papers helped the new immigrants adjust to their new life. There was information on how to become an American citizen, articles about American government and history, and regular local and international news. One daily paper called *Forwards* soon became the most important Jewish newspaper in the country. It helped workers by discussing problems in the American work force. This paper is still published today in English and Yiddish. Even though the immigrants had Yiddish newspapers, they worked hard to learn English. Many adults went to school at night.

Life was hard for the Jewish immigrants. Some Jews had to work in "sweatshops," run-down factories where clothes or other goods were made. This was one of the few jobs they could get if they didn't know English. In sweatshops, people worked in terrible conditions. Sometimes they had no electricity, no running water, and their bathrooms were filthy. They would work all day long with only a short lunch break. On top of that, they were locked into the sweatshops during the day, because the managers thought that they might take a break when they were supposed to be working. The factories were crowded, and many people got sick in the sweatshops because of all the germs. If they were sick and stayed home from work, they lost their jobs. People worked six days a week, 10 to 16 hours per day. The workers had no health insurance, sick pay, or vacations. They hardly had any time to spend with their families.

Samuel Gompers

When the Jews came to America, they were used to fighting for their rights and the rights of others. They used their leadership skills to organize the garment workers to stand up for their rights. They laid the foundation for improved working conditions for future generations.

Samuel Gompers was an important person during the forming of the American labor movement. He started the American Federation of Labor (AFL). He believed that it didn't matter where you came from or what you believed, but that all people should be treated the same. He wanted all men and women—not just Jews—to unite for better working conditions and better salaries.

Rose Schneiderman was another person who fought for better working conditions, especially for women. She organized the union called the International Ladies Garment Workers Union (ILGWU). Like the AFL, this union battled for better working conditions and higher pay for the women workers.

The Jewish people valued justice and fairness for everyone. They worked hard to change working conditions, and things improved. Work places are better and much healthier now. We are thankful that they didn't give up and that their hard-fought struggles were successful in changing the working conditions for all future American workers.

American Jews continued to read about things happening in Europe. They remembered an 1894 legal case called the Dreyfus Affair. The French Army accused Alfred Dreyfus of telling French secrets to the German Army. Alfred Dreyfus was not really guilty—the French arrested him because he was a Jew. They used made-up evidence to find him guilty.

Theodor Herzl, a reporter at the Dreyfus trial, believed Dreyfus was innocent. What bothered him the most during the trial was the crowd outside the court that kept yelling, "Down with the Jews—Death to the Jews!"

Herzl said that in Europe, "Jews do not get all the rights that non-Jews get. The Jews need their own state." After the Dreyfus case, Herzl became the founder of the Zionist Movement, which argued that the Jewish people had to reestablish a country of their own in order to be free and safe. Zionists are people who wanted to return to the Land of Israel. Many American Jews started talking about this idea, too.

There were people and organizations that didn't like Jews in America, but most Jewish Americans continued to have their civil rights. However, during the 1930s, many Americans, including the Jews, became worried about what was happening in Nazi Germany. Although many German Jews were poets, writers, musicians, artists, teachers, and scientists who had fought for Germany in World War I, their rights and their place in German life were changing. These Jewish people had done great things for Germany. Between 1905 and 1936, Jews won 14 out of the 38 Nobel Prizes

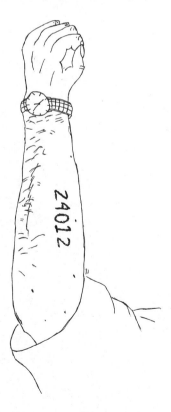

awarded in Germany. Jews were active in all aspects of German culture.

After World War I, Germany, like other countries, was going through an economic depression. Adolf Hitler convinced the people that he would get rid of their economic problems. He created the Nazi Party. He began to convince people that the Jews were responsible for many of Germany's problems, which was an outright lie. Hitler moved fast to take away the rights of the Jews. Germany passed laws taking away Jews' freedom of speech, privacy, religion, and all other civil rights. The Nazis could read people's mail, listen in on phone calls, and search homes. The "Storm Troopers" of the Nazi Party ran through the streets burning books and attacking

and murdering people, especially Jews. The situation was growing worse.

Soon all German newspapers, radios, books, magazines, art, and music were controlled by the Nazis. They burned books that they thought were against their views and should not be read. In just a single night, 25,000 books were destroyed, including those written by Jewish writers such as Albert Einstein and Sigmund Freud. Most were written by non-Jews, including famous Americans like Jack London, Ernest Hemingway, and Sinclair Lewis. Hundreds of thousands of Americans protested the book burnings, but they couldn't stop the Nazis.

The Nazis carried out a boycott against Jewish businesses, which means they told people not to buy from them. Signs were made that said "Don't buy from Jews" and "The Jews are our misfortune." Soon laws were passed that made it illegal for Jews to have businesses, teach school, travel to certain places, or work for the government. Jewish children were forbidden to attend public school. On November 9, 1938, the Germans attacked the Jewish communities and synagogues. In just two days, more than 1,000 synagogues were burned, 7,000 Jewish businesses were destroyed, dozens of Jewish people were killed, and Jewish cemeteries, hospitals, schools, and homes were robbed. The police and fire brigades did nothing. Broken glass from store windows was spread through the streets. This event became known as *Kristallnacht* (crystal-nahkt), which means "Night of the Broken Glass."

For a while, the Nazis allowed Jews to leave the country. But after 1939, they couldn't leave. Their homes were taken away, and they were moved to areas only for Jews, called "ghettos." Walls were put up to keep the Jews inside these neighborhoods. Often three or four families were forced to live in one small apartment. It was forbidden to bring food into the ghetto and many Jews starved to death. Hitler was so powerful that he could do whatever he pleased. He eventually moved the Jews to the concentration camps, which were much worse than the ghettos. He didn't want any of them to live.

In America, the Jews of New York City organized a march to protest the Nazis' rise to power in Germany. Tens of thousands of people went to New York to be a part of this protest. When Hitler came to power, Henrietta Szold, an American Jewish woman in her seventies, realized that Jewish children were in great danger. She helped to start the Youth Aliyah (ah-le-YA) Move-

Student authors studying Jewish history

ment in 1933 to help young people escape from Nazi Germany. Being part of Aliyah meant going to live in Israel, which was called Palestine at that time. The movement took German kids to Palestine by sneaking them across mountains and over seas. American Jews gave money and supplies to help this youth movement so that Jewish people could survive. Support from American Jews made it easier for these Jewish kids to adapt to their new environment.

During World War II, few Jews were brought to America because the U.S. government wouldn't let any more people come into this country. President Roosevelt ignored the pleas of Jewish Americans to change the laws that kept immigrants out. For example, in May of 1939 a ship called the S.S. *St. Louis* left Germany with 936 passengers. All but six of them were Jews. No country would let them in, and they finally arrived in America. But America wouldn't let them in either, and they were sent back to Germany. The only Jews who were saved by America during the war were famous people, like Albert Einstein. Finally, in 1944, President Roosevelt established a War Refugee Board that saved a few Jews, but it was too late for most of them.

Other Americans felt that World War II was Europe's problem and that America shouldn't get involved. Even though American troops weren't fighting early in the war, the U.S. government was sending money and military support to European countries fighting against Hitler. When the Japanese bombed Pearl Harbor in Hawaii in 1941, the United States decided to send troops to the Pacific and Europe. At that time, 500,000 Jews joined the American armed forces. They were glad their country was finally going to do more to help the Jews and other people in Europe who were suffering because of Hitler.

By the time the war was over, the Nazis had killed 11 million people. Six million of them were Jews, and over 1 million of them were children. Thankfully, the Youth Aliyah Movement had been able to save about 17,000 children by moving them from Europe to Palestine.

THE REBIRTH OF ISRAEL

After the war, the Jews continued to work hard to establish Israel. Since 1919, Pales-

tine had been a colony ruled by Britain. The Jews went to the United Nations and asked them to give them this land as their homeland. Even though Theodor Herzl was no longer alive, his work finally paid off. On May 14, 1948, Israel became a democratic state. In the past, Israel had always been considered the homeland for all Jews; now it was official. Jews all over the world now had a country to call their own.

At the same time, Jewish Americans continued to fight for civil rights in America. Jews were concerned about others not having equal rights. They wanted all people to be treated fairly. When the soldiers came home after fighting in World War II, even though they were honored as heroes, many soldiers weren't treated with respect. Some Americans were angry that the African American soldiers, who had risked their lives for our country, were not given all the rights of American citizens. They were treated like second-class citizens.

In 1965, there was a big march with thousands of people who believed that African Americans should be treated as equals. They marched from Selma to Montgomery, Alabama. Rabbi Abraham

Joshua Heschel led the march with Reverend Martin Luther King Jr., and other people. The civil rights movement held hundreds of marches all over the country and kept trying and trying to change things for African Americans.

Henry Moskowitz and Rabbi Stephen Wise helped start the civil rights movement. There were a lot of other Jewish people, such as Martha Gruening, who helped the civil rights movement by reporting on hate groups like the Ku Klux Klan. Joel Elias Spingarn and his brother Arthur were two of the first members of the National Association for the Advancement of Colored People (NAACP). Joel became the chairman of the board and later the president of the NAACP. Arthur was a lawyer who fought for laws to allow blacks and whites to attend the same schools and to live in the same neighborhoods. He was also the president of the NAACP for several years.

Meanwhile, the new state of Israel was having problems. There were several wars between Israel and the Arab nations during the 1950s, 1960s, and 1970s. At the invitation of former President Jimmy Carter, Israeli President Menachem Begin and Egyptian President Anwar Sadat agreed to have peace talks near Washington, D.C. The two leaders signed a peace treaty, and there hasn't been war between these two countries since then. But wars have continued with other countries and within Israel. The United States continues to encourage countries to make peace with Israel.

Israel has tried to make peace with its neighbors, but neither the Jews nor the Palestinians have ever gotten along well together. Many lives have been lost because of the fighting between these two groups. If there were peace in the Middle East, there wouldn't be so many disagreements over water, oil, tourism, fertile land, and people. Life would be better for everyone in the area. Now peace is closer than ever before in the Middle East, but there is still a lot of work to be done.

Today, Israel is one of the only countries that is very old and very young at the same time. Many American Jews are still involved in the Zionist movement. Israel is very important to many Jews in America because it is a reminder that a homeland exists for them if they need one. You may have heard that Israel is not a nice place to live because there has been a lot of fighting there, but it is still a beautiful land and Jews continue to hope for *shalom*—peace. For Jews, Israel is a symbol of Jewish unity and pride in their heritage.

LIVING THROUGH HISTORY

Even though World War II was a war that involved the armies and people of many nations, there was another war going on, too. It was Hitler's war against the Jews, called the *Shoah* (SHOW-ah) or Holocaust. Jewish Americans have worked very hard to share the stories from the Holocaust because they don't want people to forget the horrible things that happened. The largest Holocaust memorial museum is in Washington, D.C. There are many Holocaust exhibits and speakers traveling around the United States. These groups believe that if they can remind people of this terrible tragedy, they can stop it from happening again to anybody, anywhere in the world.

It was a terrible time when millions of Jews and other people were killed. Today, some Americans actually believe the Holocaust didn't happen. But it did happen! Our class saw the proof when one Holocaust survivor and one concentration camp liberator came to our workshop, talked to us, and showed us pictures. We have chosen to write these stories so we can do our part to help prevent this horrible injustice from happening in the future and to make people understand that it was real.

Here's what we heard from two people who lived through this part of history. These two people shared their stories with us and asked people of all ages to end their hatred and start respecting one another. As we listened to their two stories, we knew we would never forget the evil that the Nazis had done.

Bernie Sayonne

Bernie Sayonne is an American citizen who survived the brutality of World War II. He talked to us about the horrors he encountered as a Jewish teenager living in Poland. When Germany started the war with Poland, Bernie was only 17 years old. Life was never good for the Jews in Poland. He lived in a quiet town that became very different within three years. One Friday night in 1939, when all the Jews were in synagogue, Nazi troops poured gasoline all over the synagogue and burned it. Bernie lived

Bernie Sayonne

across the street from the synagogue and didn't attend that night because he had seen Nazis in town. Bernie and his family looked on helplessly from their window at what was happening.

When we asked him why his family didn't try to get away, Bernie told us that no one imagined that the Nazis would attack Poland. When the Germans took over Poland, more laws were made telling Jews what they had to do. They had to wear a yellow Star of David as a sign that they were Jewish. They all had to be in their houses by 8 p.m. They couldn't go to the public pool or schools. They couldn't even sit on the same benches with non-Jews. Fear began to build in the Jewish people. We shared this feeling of fear when we interviewed Bernie.

Soon all of the Jews were moved into a bad part of town. It had a barbed-wire fence around it. People could go in, but the Nazis would never let the Jews go out. Inside the ghetto were grocery stores with no food and schools with no teachers. Some of the people with a good education, including teachers, doctors, and lawyers, were arrested and immediately put to death.

Then one day Jews were forced onto trains meant for carrying cattle. The Nazis stuffed at least 150 people into each car. Bernie told us that people had to sleep standing up, and many died from heat exhaustion, starvation, and suffocation. They were told that the ride would take eight hours, but it took two days. The train stopped only to remove dead bodies. Bernie will never forget the horrible smell when they were at least a mile away from their destination. He told us it was indescribable, like burning rubber mixed with oil and old rags. Bernie found out later that the horrible smell was from the burning of dead bodies.

When they arrived at Auschwitz—a Nazi concentration camp in Poland—family members were separated into male and female lines, and then by age. Bernie was assigned to the job of burying bodies found in the train cars and throughout the camp. He told us that he buried hundreds of people every day. To survive, Bernie forced himself not to think about anything. He made himself function like a robot.

One day Bernie overheard a guard say that his group would be the next to die. As he entered the buildings where he slept, he saw a billboard that said the Nazis needed machinists. To keep from getting killed, he and two friends lied to the Nazis and said that they were machinists. They were not very skilled, but they knew enough to keep themselves alive. The prisoners had to stand outside naked while the Nazis checked to see if they were too sick to work or had any small injuries. If they did, they were killed.

Planes bombed the factory where Bernie worked, so he was sent back to Auschwitz. Bernie and 19 others then became part of a horrible medical experiment. Nazi doctors injected them with typhus—a terrible disease. Only he and one other man survived.

Finally, the Allied Forces defeated the German forces and set the prisoners free. When Bernie was 21 years old, he weighed only 67 pounds. He had been separated from his family since the beginning of the war. At the end of the war, only his younger brother and he had survived. Two years later, after getting married and starting a family, Bernie came to America.

Today Bernie feels proud that he has been able to raise his children and grandchildren in a free country. He is proud to be an American citizen and to live in a nation where he can vote, and where people are not judged by their race or their religion.

"If even half the people in America felt as fortunate as I do to live in our country," Bernie told us, "America would be an even better place to live." He encouraged all of us to get involved with our country, because

Bernie hopes people will learn how to respect one another, and we do, too!

Felix Sparks

Like Bernie Sayonne, General Felix Sparks wants people to know that the Holocaust really happened. When he was young, Felix Sparks—a Christian college student from Colorado—wanted to be a lawyer. He didn't have enough money to continue to pay for college, so he joined the Army. In World War II, his brigade invaded Nazi Germany. He served in the U.S. Army for many years and became a brigadier general.

General Sparks' troops were sent to invade the city of Munich, then later they were told to take over Dachau Concentration Camp. General Sparks and his troops didn't know what to expect. First, they came to a long line of about 39 train cars that were lined up outside the camp. They found more than 2,000 dead bodies in the train cars. The American soldiers were disgusted with what they saw. Some had to look away, and others cried or got sick.

You might think these soldiers were used to death since it is a part of war. But this was just too overwhelming because the people who died were just innocent citizens and had been killed in such awful ways. The men never got used to the smells or sights of the concentration camps.

General Sparks ordered his troops to climb over the wall and take over the concentration camp. Many of the Nazi troops surrendered. Those who put up a fight were killed. After the Nazi troops were captured, the American soldiers went into the place where the prisoners were held.

General Felix Sparks

They saw dead bodies everywhere. There were about 15,000 people who were still alive, but they were weak and sick. In one part of the camp was a building that had the ovens where the dead bodies were burned. In a room next to the ovens, bodies were stacked high, waiting to be burned.

General Sparks forced the citizens of the town of Dachau to help bury the bodies in huge ditches. He did this to make the citizens see what had happened right near their town. General Sparks knew the survivors needed medical help, and so doctors and nurses got there in two days. But even with medicine, 200 people died every day for the first few months because they had many diseases.

After the war, General Sparks finished law school and got a job as a lawyer. Later, he was appointed to the Supreme Court of the State of Colorado. After a while, he started speaking at schools, on TV, and on the radio about what he had seen. He felt strongly that people need to be reminded of what happened in Nazi Germany.

General Sparks told us some important things. He said that hatred of others is destructive. There is nothing worse than hating another human being. Hate groups don't do anything but create hate and misery, so he told us to stay away from them and not get tricked into believing them. He wants us to respect all people and work together with them so that every person has a right to live and worship the way he or she chooses. Respecting the beliefs of other people means allowing them to practice their beliefs freely.

From our speakers, we learned we can't change the mistakes of the past. But we can learn from these mistakes and do our part to make sure they don't happen again. By doing this, we can affect what will happen in the future!

in just a few pages since the Jews have been around for over 4,000 years, and that's twice as old as most civilizations. Numerous times people have tried to destroy the Jews, but somehow the Jews have always pulled through. The Jewish people have managed to survive in many places around the world.

Throughout Jewish history, Jews have struggled hard to keep their heritage alive. The beginning of their history is recorded in the first five books of the Bible—Genesis, Exodus, Leviticus, Numbers, and Deuteronomy. The Hebrew word for the Bible is *Tanach*, and the first five books are called the *Torah* (TOR-ah). The *Talmud* (TAHL-mood) is the oral Torah. The telling and retelling of these stories have been part of how the Jewish people have kept their ancient history alive. You might be surprised to find out that you have already learned a lot about Jewish history from reading the Old Testament Bible stories. These stories are the history of the Jewish people.

JEWISH HISTORY: ANCIENT TIMES TO THE TWENTIETH CENTURY

This is the third part of our history chapter, which discusses the years before Jewish immigrants came to America. The Jewish people came to this country with a long history, and we didn't want to leave that out. It's almost impossible to tell the story

Angel of death

Jewish people have lived in many places and have had many names. You will read about them as Hebrews, Israelites, Judeans, and Jews. Also, the land of Israel has been known by many other names, such as Canaan, Judea, and Palestine. While you read about Jewish history before America, you will see the term B.C.E. ("before the common era") in place of B.C. ("before Christ"). You will also see the term C.E. ("common era") in place of A.D. ("Anno Domini"), which means "in the year of the Lord Christ." Jewish people record their history this way, so we have done the same thing in our book.

Jews and their culture have survived because of their strong faith in G-d, traditions, and education. Jewish ancestors have conquered and have been conquered. Over their long history, the Jews have helped many cultures become successful.

Abraham (1900 B.C.E.)

Abram believed that there had always been one G-d. Abram was chosen to create a nation of holy people for G-d, who gave Abram the new name of Abraham. G-d had taken Abram and added a "hey" from the word *hamon*, which means "many" in Hebrew. *Ab* (Av) in Hebrew stands for "father." So Abram became Abraham, which means "father of many people."

Abraham trusted G-d so much that he was willing to go to a new land. He is considered the father of the Jewish people.

Jacob and Esau (1750 B.C.E.)

Isaac was the son of Abraham. Isaac and his wife, Rebecca, had twins, Jacob and Esau. Jacob's 12 sons became the leaders of the Israelites, who later became known as the Jewish people. Later, one of Jacob's sons, Joseph, saved his brothers and their families from starvation by letting them come to Egypt. Then the kind pharaoh, who liked Joseph, died and a new pharaoh, who hated the Hebrews, came into power.

Becoming a Nation (1450–1410 B.C.E.)

For 400 years, the Hebrews were forced to be slaves to the pharaoh in Egypt. G-d spoke to Moses from a burning bush and told him to rescue the Israelites from Egypt. Then G-d punished the pharaoh and the Egyptians with ten plagues, and Moses led the Hebrew slaves out of Egypt. When they came to the Red Sea, Moses lifted his rod and the sea separated so the Israelites could safely cross on dry land. After the Israelites reached the other side, the water came back together and drowned the Egyptians who were chasing them. Jews remember this time in history when they celebrate Passover. You can read more about Passover in the Holidays chapter.

While the Hebrews were in the desert, they gathered at Mount Sinai to receive the Torah and the Ten Commandments. The Torah is the written story of the early Israelites as well as a guide for how Jews should live. When they got the Ten Commandments, they began to develop into a "nation" even though they had no land yet. Moses passed down the Oral Tradition, the words that helped the people understand the Torah. These laws, customs, and traditions helped unify the Hebrews as a people. During this time, the Hebrews accepted their agreement with G-d to be His people.

Before Moses died, Joshua was chosen to be the new leader of G-d's people. When G-d told them to take possession of Canaan, Joshua had the people pray for a plan from G-d. The plan was strange, but they believed G-d anyway. The Hebrews marched around the city of Jericho day after day. After seven days, they were singing and blowing their trumpets when the walls of Jericho came tumbling down! It was their first battle in their new land, and Joshua and the Jewish people won.

After Moses and Joshua died, there were other leaders. These leaders were called the "judges." They helped the people make decisions, solve problems, and acted as generals during their wars. One of the most famous judges was Deborah. She was the leader for 40 years. During this time, Deborah led her people to many victories. It took more than 200 years before all of the promised land of Canaan was finally in the hands of the Israelites.

The Kings (1050–933 B.C.E.)

After the period of the judges, the Jews wanted a king because they saw that all

their neighbors had one. Samuel, a priest and Jewish leader, went looking for a king and found Saul. Saul won many of the wars with the help of Samuel. But Saul also did many things that made G-d and Samuel angry. So G-d helped Samuel choose King David. He was a brilliant general and a mighty conqueror. He was also a musician who wrote psalms, which are poetic songs written in praise of G-d. King David was Israel's leader during its "Golden Age."

King Solomon, who was known for his great wisdom, became the third King of Israel. He built the First Temple and placed the Holy Ark there. This was where the Torah was kept. King Solomon made treaties and helped the land of Israel grow rich. King Solomon's Temple was destroyed by the Babylonians in 586 B.C.E.

Rabbinic Times (586 B.C.E.–135 C.E.)

In the days of the rabbis, many of the Jews had to live without a temple or their own land. This is how the Talmud developed. The Talmud is Jewish laws and stories. During this period, the book called the *Ethics of the Fathers* was written so that Jews could learn in more detail how G-d wanted them to act. It teaches that the world is based on three principles: the Torah, the worship of one G-d, and being kind and loving.

Greeks (168–164 B.C.E.)

Over time, Jews were persecuted by different people and nations. Many rulers felt that the G-d of the Jews was a threat to the authority of the king. They were afraid the Jews would get too strong and powerful. Jews were forced to accept the ways of their conquerors or face exile, destruction, or even death.

One way to crush the spirit of the Jews was to force them to bow down to idols. Many Jewish people died because they wouldn't worship anyone or anything but their G-d, who had no human form. No one knew what G-d looked like.

One Jewish woman, Hannah, had seven sons who refused to bow down to an evil king and were killed. The seventh son was only three years old, so the king thought he could trick him into bowing down. The king threw his ring down and thought the seventh son would bend over to pick it up, which would be similar to bowing to the idol. Instead of picking it up, the seventh son kicked the ring back to the king. The seventh son was killed, too. They all died for their faith. Jews remember these events each year when they celebrate *Hanukkah* (HAH-nuh-kah). The

Holidays chapter tells more about the story of Hanukkah.

Romans (538 B.C.E.)

When the Jews of the Babylonian exile came back to Judea, they built the Holy Temple for the second time. It was not as big or as beautiful as the First Temple. In 63 B.C.E., to please the Jews and to impress the Romans, Herod added more to the Temple to make it as beautiful as possible. He also built many palaces in Israel. One was built on the top of a hill called Masada. The Romans made Herod the king of Judea. The Jews, though, didn't really like Herod because he put Roman idols in the Holy Temple instead of keeping it holy.

Jerusalem:
Destruction of Second Temple
and Masada (70–100 C.E.)

In 70 C.E., the Roman General Titus had the Roman soldiers burn down the Temple, but the Western Wall remained standing. It is still there for us to see today. This wall is also known as the *Kotel*, or the "Wailing Wall." Today, the Wailing Wall is a very important sight in Jerusalem. Many people from all over the world come here to pray. Some kids even have their Bar Mitzvah at the Wall. People write little notes and stick them in the cracks for G-d to read. One side of the wall is for men and the other side is for women.

After the destruction of the Second Temple in the year 70 C.E., a small group of Jewish fighters called Zealots and their families hid from the Romans on Masada—a mountain fortress. Meanwhile, the Romans tried to capture the people living on Masada. After holding out for three years, the Zealots felt that they would rather die as free people than become slaves, so they killed their wives and children, and then themselves. When the Romans climbed up to Masada, they found only dead bodies. They had won, but they were never able to capture the Zealots as slaves.

Although the Romans destroyed the Second Temple, the Roman period was a time when Jewish law was expanded and written down. Some rabbis began to organize the Oral Law of the Talmud. The Talmud is made up of the *Mishnah* and *Gemara*. These are interpretations of the Torah, laws, and stories. The laws in the Talmud teach Jews how to act toward one another and the world around them—and to be sensitive to the rights of all people. Even though the Jews were spread out and sent to different places, they all had similar beliefs and practices. Even today, Jews study the Torah and use the Talmud to help understand how to make themselves better people.

Middle Ages (500–1492 C.E.)

Throughout the Middle Ages and most of history, Jewish people were treated very poorly. The governments of Europe and the Catholic Church didn't like the Jews. Many Europeans thought Jews were inferior and forced them to wear special badges, to pay special taxes, and to give up their religion. They were forced to live apart from their Christian neighbors. They couldn't own land and have certain jobs. It was a hard time for the Jewish people.

Golden Age of Spain (950–1100 C.E.)

In 756 C.E., part of Spain broke away from the rest of the Muslim Empire and set up their own independent state. From the start, the newly formed Muslim state allowed the Jews to practice their religion freely with few restrictions. How good this must have felt! Although Jews had to pay special taxes, they continued to build syna-

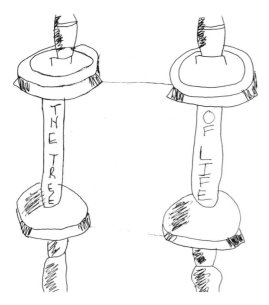

gogues, homes, and schools. They were able to become doctors, philosophers, writers, politicians, and even soldiers.

A Jew named Moses Maimonides was a doctor, a philosopher, and a rabbi. He wrote many books. In his book called *The Guide for the Perplexed*, he tried to prove that the Torah could fit well with science and philosophy. Another of his books was the *Mishnah Torah*. In that book, he took the legal material from the Talmud, summed it up, and rearranged it so that it was easy to understand and use. Some people even compared Maimonides to Moses, because he brought the teaching of G-d to the people of Israel in a way that they could understand.

The Spanish Inquisition (1300–1500 C.E.)

Prejudice against the Jews spread rapidly throughout all Europe. In 1492, Queen Isabella wanted Spain to be an all-Christian

land. She tried to force Jews to become Catholic. This time was called the Spanish Inquisition. Many Jews were forced to convert to Christianity, but some still practiced Judaism in secret and were called *Marranos* or *Conversos*. Nonbelievers were sometimes executed, so many Jews left Spain to escape the Spanish Inquisition.

At this time, Columbus was planning his trip to the new land. Some people believe that if it hadn't been for Jewish map makers, Columbus never would have found America. Many think Conversos were crew members on the boat with the famous explorer and that Columbus himself might even have been a Converso. There are some ancestors of Conversos still living in the southwestern part of the United States. These people are Catholics, but have some Jewish customs that their families have practiced for generations.

The Reformation Through Emancipation (1500–1800 C.E.)

The Reformation, which Martin Luther started in the 1500s, was a time when Protestants became stronger and wanted the Jews to convert to their kind of Christianity. When the Jews refused, the Protestants persecuted them just as the Catholic Church had done. Even though this was a difficult time for the Jews, Jewish learning continued to grow.

Much later, in the 1700s, two Jewish movements developed. One was the Jewish Enlightenment and the other was the Chassidic Movement. The Chassidim encouraged people to worship G-d with prayer, song, and dance.

During the Jewish Enlightenment movement, Germany became more tolerant of different kinds of people. Opportunities for Jews appeared in education and in business. The "Enlightened" Jews wanted to prove that they could be accepted as equals in the country. About this time, Jews began arriving in America.

This is only part of the history that Jewish people brought with them to America. This history has helped make the Jews strong. It has also helped them survive and prosper despite many persecutions. It also explains why certain traditions are still very important to the Jewish people today.

Remember, there are many wonderful books that discuss Jewish history and have much more information in them. We hope you will go to the library and read some more. After all, the Jews are often called "The People of the Book!"

GROWING UP JEWISH

There are people to learn from,
There are life cycles to know.
When you study Jewish heritage,
Then the more you will grow.

In this chapter, we talk about what it is like for children and young adults to grow up Jewish. Growing up Jewish might be a little different, but it is similar to other cultures in many ways.

This chapter has two parts. First, explore the Jewish life cycle, or the "rites of passage," which are the ways people celebrate being Jewish. Read about birth, *Bar* and *Bat* (baht) *Mitzvahs*, weddings, and deaths and what happens when these occur in a Jewish person's life. Some events involve important family gatherings that have been going on for generations, carrying on Jewish traditions. These celebrations make the rites of passage enjoyable for children as well as adults. The second part of this chapter reveals traditions

young Jewish people have in their lives. Learn about young people from across America and how they use mitzvot to make our world a better place.

Mitzvot (mits-VOTE) are a big part of being Jewish. Mitzvot, which means "obligation" in Hebrew, are good deeds and commandments handed down from G-d and written in the Torah. At different times in their lives, Jews are commanded to perform certain mitzvot. There are 613 different mitzvot and they are all written in the Torah. For example, there are mitzvot for births, weddings, deaths, baths, and fasting days. There is even a mitzvah that tells people that they must feed their animals before they eat a meal. Laws give Jews guidance on almost every issue.

BIRTH

Mazel tov! In Hebrew, this means "Congratulations!" A lot of American Jews say this when a baby is born. The beginning of the Jewish life cycle starts with a new life. The first celebration in the baby's life is usually when the child gets a name. Some parents name the baby after a family member who has died so that they will remember a relative they loved. The parents can choose a name for their child by themselves or have a rabbi name the baby. Often the baby is given a Hebrew name as well as an English name. These celebrations are different for boys and girls.

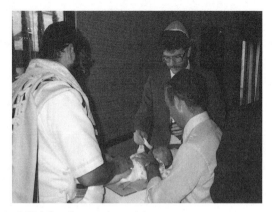

A Mohel performs a circumcision

For a Baby Boy

Mazel tov! It's a boy!

The first ceremony in a Jewish boy's life is the *brit milah* (brit MEE-lah). The brit is the covenant, or the agreement, between Abraham, the father of Judaism, and G-d. Jewish people believe Abraham was commanded by G-d to circumcise himself and his sons as a sign of his devotion to G-d. Since that time, most Jewish families have followed this custom. Circumcision is performed on most American baby boys right after birth, but in the Jewish religion, it's an important ritual.

The brit is performed by a trained circumcisor called a *Mohel* (MO-hel) when the baby boy is eight days old. It happens on the eighth day because that is what is commanded in the Torah. If you go to a brit, this is what might happen. First, the baby is carried in by his G-dparents. Sometimes the parents choose a Jewish couple who don't have children yet in order to bring the couple good luck. Then the Mohel picks up the baby and says a prayer. The Mohel carefully removes the foreskin of the boy's penis with a knife. (Ouch! But babies don't remember this.) After the ceremony, some families celebrate with good Jewish food or by having a party at home.

For a Baby Girl

Mazel tov! It's a girl!

The first ceremony for a Jewish baby girl is commonly called a "baby-naming." Some Jews also call this celebration a *Simchat Bat* ("celebration of a daughter") or even a *Shalom Nekaivah* ("Hello, Female!"). Baby-namings are traditionally done in the synagogue on Saturday, Monday, or Thursday mornings when the Torah is removed from the ark. These ceremonies are religious, and some Jewish Americans say blessings and prayers to make the baby-naming more meaningful. Most Jewish girls are named soon after they are born. In the synagogue, the father and mother may be called up in front of the congregation.

Someone will read from the Torah, and then a prayer is said over the baby. At last-the baby's name is announced. Afterwards, the family will have a feast either in the synagogue or at home.

Pidyon Haben

Orthodox Jewish families hold the *pidyon haben* (PID-yon ha-BEN), or redemption ceremony. It is mostly Orthodox Jews who have this ceremony because the Torah says that the first-born son belongs to G-d until he is redeemed by his family. This ceremony is also done to remember the Egyptians' first-born sons who were sacrificed when the first-born sons of the Jewish people were spared during the first Passover. The word redemption means "buying back." The family of the newborn gives special coins to the *kohen* (KO-hane), who is considered a direct descendant of Moses and Aaron, in exchange for their firstborn son.

The ceremony is held 31 days after the first son is born. He is placed on a special tray and presented to the kohen. The father says a special phrase that tells the kohen the baby is his first son, and to keep his baby the father must give the kohen five *shekels* (SHEH-kels). A shekel is a silver coin which was used in Israel, but today many American Jews use five silver dollars. Then the kohen holds the money over the baby's head and says that the exchange is accepted.

Don't worry. Even if a Jewish family does not do the ceremony, the kohen won't keep the baby! The pidyon haben is just a Jewish tradition.

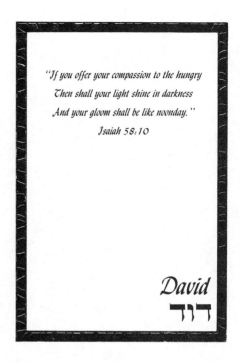

"If you offer your compassion to the hungry
Then shall your light shine in darkness
And your gloom shall be like noonday."
Isaiah 58:10

David
דוד

BAR AND BAT MITZVAHS

Bar is the word for "son" and *bat* is the word for "daughter." A Bar or Bat Mitzvah means "son or daughter of the commandment." The Bar or Bat Mitzvah is an event that celebrates the time when a Jewish boy or girl becomes a responsible adult in the eyes of the Jewish community. The ceremony is a public commitment to one's Judaism.

Many Jewish American children go to Hebrew school when they are young so they can study their faith and learn the *alef-bet* (Hebrew alphabet) in preparation for their Bar or Bat Mitzvah. Jewish people feel that it is important to study their faith as well as regular subjects like reading and math.

Two authors wearing prayer shawls and yalmulkes

Bar Mitzvah

When a Jewish boy turns 13, he is considered a grown-up in the Jewish religion. A Jewish American boy prepares for his Bar Mitzvah by studying Hebrew very hard because he may be allowed to read a portion from the Torah during the ceremony. He is also encouraged to give a speech which usually includes an explanation of his Torah portion and his feelings about the message.

One really great part of a Bar Mitzvah is the party! A Bar Mitzvah party might be about ten times as big as a normal birthday party. The boy might get lots of presents like watches and *kipot* (KEY-poot), which are a type of hat. Some families hire musicians and entertainers. Sometimes they have caterers serve the food. This is what one Reform Jewish American boy thought about his upcoming Bar Mitzvah: "It seems my family is so involved in the party planning that I have to remind myself that a Bar Mitzvah is not just a party, but is something that lasts an entire lifetime. I think that once the day is over I will feel that I accomplished something. I know I will walk away with great memories. I hope my Bar Mitzvah day will highlight spiritual aspects. This will turn the day into an important personal experience."

On or before his Bar Mitzvah, an Orthodox Jewish American boy begins wearing *tefillin* (tah-FILL-in) while he says his morning prayers. Tefillin are two black boxes with prayers inside that are attached to long leather straps. One is worn on the forehead and one is worn on the arm he doesn't write with. He might also begin to wear a *tallit* (tah-LEET), which is a prayer shawl. The tallit is a rectangular piece of cloth that has four sets of long fringes, which represent the four corners of the universe that G-d created. When counted together, the knots of the fringes themselves add up to 613, the number of commandments, or mitzvot, in the Torah.

"Since my Bar Mitzvah, it has become more important for me to pray," said one Orthodox Jewish boy about his new responsibilities. "I now put on tefillin and pray every morning. Prayer is important to me because it has given me something I can do for G-d."

Bat Mitzvah

Bat Mitzvahs were started in the 1920s by a rabbi who had only daughters. Jewish American girls usually have a Bat Mitzvah between the ages of 12 and 13. This ceremony happens so Jewish friends and family can celebrate with a girl who has become a grown-up member of the Jewish community. At this time, she accepts all the commandments and the Jewish law considers her a woman.

This is what one Orthodox Jewish American girl said about her life after her Bat Mitzvah: "Two weeks after my Bat

Mitzvah, I had a fast day. It started at sunrise and ended at sundown. Also, now I can't touch a boy and a boy cannot touch me. Before my Bat Mitzvah, I could wear pants, but now I don't. I wear skirts to be more modest and all my shirts have sleeves. I also try not to attract attention to myself. I think Jewish modesty laws help men and women respect each other more."

If the girl is not Orthodox, she might read from the Torah. An Orthodox girl usually gives a speech about something she recently learned. Most Bat Mitzvah girls have a party. Usually only women come to an Orthodox girl's Bat Mitzvah party, but both men and women go to a Conservative or Reform Bat Mitzvah party.

Some Jewish women who didn't have a Bat Mitzvah when they were young are now having it later in their lives. Bat Mitzvahs started to become more and more popular in America as our culture saw that girls had an equally important place in society. Wouldn't you like to go to a Bat Mitzvah and celebrate, too?

MARRIAGE

Many Jewish men and women do not consider themselves "whole" until they get married. Getting married also fulfills one of the mitzvot. The mitzvah from the Torah reads, "And the Lord G-d said it is not good that man should be alone." Getting married is the first step toward forming a new Jewish family to pass on Jewish traditions.

Engagements

Long ago many Orthodox Jewish parents chose husbands or wives for their children. Sometimes, instead of the parents making the choice, they would hire a matchmaker who would find a husband or wife for their child. If the match didn't lead to marriage, or if the two people didn't like each other, the matchmaker would try again. In the modern Orthodox tradition, Jews sometimes still use a matchmaker to help them find a spouse, but the final choice is made by the couple. Most Conservative and Reform Jewish Americans find their own partners to marry without assistance from a matchmaker.

Weddings

On the Sabbath before the wedding in the Jewish traditions, the bride, groom, and families go to the synagogue. There the groom is honored with an *aliyah* (AH-lee-AH) (being called up to the Torah). During the ceremony, the community throws candy at the engaged couple to wish them a "sweet life."

A Jewish bride and groom stand under the chupah

In Orthodox tradition, instead of meeting on the Sabbath before the wedding, the bride and groom can't see each other for the whole week before the wedding. An Orthodox bride also takes a special spiritual bath called a *mikvah* (MIK-vuh) before the big day. On their wedding day, the bride and groom fast until after the wedding.

Many Jewish American weddings are more similar to traditional American weddings. Some Jewish American weddings are a mixture of American and Orthodox Jewish weddings. The groom wears a white robe called a *kittel* (kit-TIL). He walks down the aisle either with his parents or the two fathers of the couple. The groom stands under the *chupah* (HOO-pa), the wedding canopy. The bride wears a white gown and a veil. She walks with her parents or both mothers of the couple. When she gets to the chupah, she walks around the groom seven times to remember the seven wedding blessings.

The chupah shelters the Jewish couple while they are getting married. It is usually decorated with flowers and represents the new house they will live in. It reminds them G-d is still above them and they have to follow the mitzvot. This is also why many Jews wear a head covering.

During the ceremony the groom usually gives the bride a ring, placing it on her right index finger. The rabbi reads the wedding vows. The bride and groom have already chosen seven special men to say the seven wedding blessings, and these men come forward now to recite them. The bride and groom drink wine from one cup to show they are joined together. The groom also stomps on a glass to remind them of the destroyed Jewish temples and that good things can follow something broken. Afterward, the congregation yells, *"Mazel tov!"*

During the week after the wedding, relatives have dinner parties for the bride and groom every night for seven days. The seven blessings that were said at the wedding ceremony are said every night at the end of each dinner party. It is a mitzvah to entertain the bride and groom, so people enjoy having these parties.

Divorce

Many Jewish Americans live happily ever after. Others do not. To be divorced in America, a Jewish couple must get both a civil and a Jewish divorce. For a civil divorce, the couple goes to a regular judge. For a Jewish divorce, the couple goes to a rabbi. The Jewish divorce document is called a *get.* Jewish law does not encourage divorces, but people are allowed to get them if they want to.

DEATH AND FUNERALS

Jews believe that people live on in the memory of others by remembering the good things about a person who died. It is a great honor to be one of the *Chevra Kadisha* (KEV-rah kah-DISH-ah), the people who are responsible for taking care of the dead. It is one of the greatest mitzvot because the dead person can never repay this good deed.

Traditionally, the body is never left alone because the Chevra Kadisha ("Holy Fellowship") want to respect and protect it. They also try to leave it as natural as possible. They do not preserve the body, so a Jewish funeral usually takes place within 24 hours after the death, unless that day is a sacred day. The body is washed because they want to return it to the earth as it arrived here. The Chevra Kadisha wrap the body in cloth, not in fancy clothes. This cloth has no pockets because nothing the person owned is as valuable as the soul. The person's prayer shawl is buried with the body. Jewish coffins are made of very plain wood and, in America, soil from Israel is sometimes put into the coffin.

If the person who died is a very close relative—such as a mother, father, sister, brother, husband, or wife—the mourners wear a black ribbon or cut their clothes near their hearts to show they feel something has been torn from their hearts. The funeral is usually not very long and sometimes it takes place near the grave. A rabbi leads the funeral and there are prayers. They talk about the person's life. The mourners recite the *kaddish* (kah-DISH), which is a prayer to remind the mourners about the goodness of G-d. After the coffin has been lowered into the grave, anyone can throw a handful of dirt on top of it. This is to show that the person has returned to the earth, the place where we all come from. Before the family returns to their house and goes in, they will wash their hands to wash away the sadness.

After the funeral is over, the mourners eat a meal that includes hard-boiled eggs, because they are a symbol of life. The family "sits *shivah*" (SHEH-vah) for three or seven days, which means they stay at home unless their mourning is interrupted by a special holiday. A special candle is lit that burns in the house for every day of mourning, and each day at sundown special prayers are said. The mourners also cover all the mirrors in their house so they don't think about themselves. People come to the house and bring lots of food for the family to eat so they don't have to cook.

Some Jewish American people wait to put a tombstone on the grave until about a year after the funeral. Then they have a small ceremony called an "unveiling." The tombstones usually have a Jewish symbol and some Hebrew words on them. Many

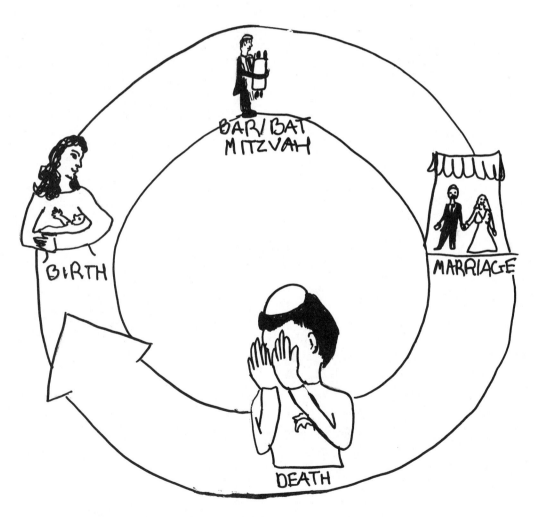

This drawing shows the events that mark the Jewish life cycle

Jewish American people have Jewish cemeteries or parts of other cemeteries that are set aside only for them.

Family members visit the grave anytime, and many say special prayers while they are visiting. Sometimes they hold a small rock in their hand while they say their prayers and then leave the small rock or a pebble on the tombstone. This is a symbol of a piece of their own spirit at the grave with their loved one, and it lets the next visitor know that the person who died is remembered. Honoring the dead is important in Judaism.

Every year on the anniversary of the person's death, the family says special prayers and lights a special candle called a *yahrzeit* (yor-TSIGHT) candle, which means "year's time." This candle burns in the family's front room window for 24 hours as a reminder of the death to all those who see it.

YOUNG PEOPLE

Making the world better for the rest,
These young people do their best.
They share in all their Jewish ways,
Working hard for better days.

Jewish kids have fun, hardships, and great times, and they celebrate a rich culture and heritage. The four kids we interviewed and wrote about have had lots of different experiences. Each of them has practiced *mitzvot*—the spirit of giving.

ASHLEY BLACK

What type of things did you enjoy when you were ten years old? Did you like to ride your bike or go to movies? When you were ten did you ever think that you could change things in society and make laws? Most of us have never done anything like that. But Ashley Black has. Ashley Black is a young Jewish American girl who has made a difference and believes that anyone can do great things, no matter how young or how old. She says that if you want to try to change something, do it! You have nothing to lose—and you might even make a difference.

Ashley is 14 years old now, but one day when she was ten, her mother told her not to watch a certain news story. Ashley usually listens to her mom, but this time her curiosity got the better of her. She watched the news program and saw a report about Nazi video games being played in Europe. That news story changed her life. It made Ashley upset because the games were so hateful toward Jewish people. The point of the games was to put Jews in concentration camps and kill them. The games made fun of people who had gone through terrible things. She thought that video games should be fun and educational, not about hate, racism, and prejudice. Ashley wondered why this game was teaching people to lead a more prejudiced life. She said we can't grow up prejudiced because we don't have enough time to hate. We all have to learn to live with each other and love each other.

So Ashley decided to do something about the video game. Ashley knew that she could make a difference by finding a way to stop these games from coming into New Jersey, where she lives. Ashley's parents have always taught her to stand up for what she believes in. With the support of her parents and lots of help from her little brother and best friend, Jeremy, Ashley started a petition drive to get signatures from people who agreed with her. With the help of volunteers, Ashley got 2,000 signatures in just two weeks! Because she worked so hard, Ashley got to meet with lawmakers to convince them to write two new laws to stop the games from being sold. People who are caught with these games in the United States now have to pay a fine, learn about the Holocaust, or go to jail.

Ashley has won many awards. She was the first winner of the Reebok Human Rights Youth in Action Award and received a $5,000 scholarship. This award was created because of what she had accomplished at such a young age. At the awards ceremony, she met former President Jimmy Carter and other famous people who are involved in human rights. Ashley was also honored at her local Jewish Community Center, receiving the Woman of Influence Award. She has been on national TV shows like "Nick News," "CBS Morning News," and MTV's "The Week in Rock."

Ashley admires people who live life to the fullest and take a stand for what they

Ashley poses with her grandparents and her brother Jeremy

Ashley Black stands with former President Jimmy Carter

believe. Ashley has many hobbies. She sings, dances, and acts, and she loves to in-line skate and help her community. She is the chairperson of community service in her Jewish youth group and volunteers at a hospital, helping others who aren't as lucky as she is. In the future, Ashley would like to arrange food and clothing drives for homeless people and do volunteer work at nursing homes.

Ashley wants children of today to realize that they are the future, and everyone needs to help make this world a safe and better place. She believes what the former Prime Minister of Israel, Golda Meir, once said—"Nothing in life just happens. It isn't enough to believe in something. You have to have the stamina to meet obstacles and overcome them—to struggle."

LEVI MARK

"Judaism to me is like water to a fish. I need it to survive. I live on it. It's my life."

Levi Mark is an Orthodox Jew. He always wears a skullcap called a *yarmulke* (YAH-muhl-kuh) and *tzitzit* (tsi-tsi), which are fringes that hang on the outside of his clothing. Levi's dad is a rabbi, his mom works for the Allied Jewish Federation, and he has three brothers. Levi believes in his religion and wants to practice it everyday.

Levi's family has always believed that being educated about Judaism is important. They wanted Levi to go to a Jewish day school instead of a regular public school so he could learn about his heritage. This didn't happen, though, because Levi had learning problems in his new school. He has dyslexia, which made it difficult for him to learn to read.

Levi's parents decided that it was more important for him to get help reading, so they put him in a school that helps children with learning disabilities. It was not a Jewish school, but the people were very nice and respected his Jewish customs. He stayed there three years before he went back to his Jewish day school. Even at his old school, he had a tutor who helped him learn Hebrew. Levi even got to skip fourth grade because he caught up so well with his studies. When he turned 13, he had his Bar Mitzvah and made everyone proud when he read aloud from the Haftorah in Hebrew.

On June 14, 1995, Levi graduated from the eighth grade at the Jewish day school. He decided to attend a Jewish high school away from his home because he wants to learn more about his religious beliefs. Levi will live at school and come home for the holidays and summer break. He wants to go to college and become a psychologist when he grows up.

Levi enjoys doing many different things outside of school. He is a member of the only Jewish Boy Scout troop in Colorado. He began Boy Scouts in first grade and is close to reaching his goal of becoming an Eagle Scout. Levi said that it is fun to be in a Jewish troop because the other members share his beliefs. The troop observes *Shabbat* (shah-BAHT, "the Sabbath") and keeps *kosher* (KOH-sher). This means that they eat only certain foods prepared in a certain way. Levi also enjoys building models, cooking, hiking, and camping. He studies and learns Jewish text with his father.

We asked Levi what his message to others would be. This is what he told us: "Growing up Jewish is different from growing up as something else. Sometimes I feel like I have missed out because I can't eat pepperoni pizza or go out for dinner wherever I want, since most restaurants aren't kosher. But my religion is more important to me than those things. Being an Orthodox Jew

Levi Mark (right) teaches kids about the Torah

A menorah

means that Judaism is a part of my everyday life, from what I wear to what I eat."

Levi also said that you should never stop learning. There is always something more to learn in life.

ELLEN LIPSTEIN

Ellen Lipstein is an 18-year-old who strives for high achievement in school and in her religion. When Ellen graduated from a public high school in 1995, she had the highest grade point average in her class. She has taken trips to Washington, D.C., New York, and Israel.

Ellen was raised as a Reform Jew near Denver, Colorado. She went to public schools and to religious and Hebrew school once a week. She studied hard for her Bat Mitzvah, which took place three days after her 13th birthday. Her celebration was very simple. She wanted to keep the focus on her religion.

Ellen also takes part in her temple youth group. Ellen was the vice president for her temple's group. For this job, she was in charge of the youth group's religious activities and even wrote the services used during their programs. She and another person were in charge of organizing a meeting for Jewish kids to meet other Jewish kids from seven states.

Ellen's favorite memory is when she was at a national conference in Washington, D.C., and participated in a service at the Lincoln Memorial! She was proud to celebrate her heritage in one of our country's historic places. Ellen is proud to be an American and to live in a country where people have freedom of religion and the right to vote.

Ellen focuses her life on helping others who are less fortunate. She lives by the

Ellen Lipstein

Golden Rule, which says to treat other people the way you would like to be treated. Ellen knew she wanted to help the needy and has tried to find many ways to do that. She organized a sock drive and helped gather and donate more than 400 pairs of socks! Ellen also has a *tzedakahm* (tsa-da-KAHM) box—a charity box she keeps in her room. At the end of every day, she takes all the change out of her pockets and puts it in the box. Whenever the box gets full, she donates it to charity.

During Ellen's summer breaks, she taught art and sports classes at the Jewish Community Center day camp. Ellen earned a scholarship to leadership camp the summer before eleventh grade. At the leadership camp, Ellen learned that it's great to be a leader and to take charge, but you also have to know when to step back and let others have a chance to lead, too. Ellen learned that even though she didn't set out to be a leader, her goals have helped her become one. She started at Brandeis University in Massachusetts in the fall of 1995. Her goal someday is to become a doctor or a rabbi.

One of Ellen's best memories about growing up Jewish was her six-week trip to Israel. Ellen said Israel was special to her because it made her a more spiritual person. She hopes everyone will have a chance to go to Israel. All people, whether they are Jewish or not, can appreciate the beauty and history of Israel.

Once, a boy told Ellen he was surprised that she was Jewish because she didn't look Jewish. Ellen thought what he said was silly because all Jewish people don't look alike. In high school, Ellen really hoped her friend would ask her to their prom, but he didn't. Later, she found out that he didn't think it was the right thing to do because they had different religions. Ellen was sad because she thinks going to dances doesn't have anything to do with religion.

Ellen has learned that it is important that no matter what your religion, you should be proud of who you are and what your beliefs are. She also says you should stand up for what you believe, but you shouldn't force your beliefs on others.

DAN ARIEL

When you're Jewish, you might hope that once during your lifetime you will have the

Dan Ariel

chance to go to Israel. Dan Ariel is a 15-year-old Conservative Jew who has already taken eight trips to Israel!

Dan, his brother, and their parents live in Denver, Colorado. An interesting thing about his parents is that his dad is from Israel and his mom's family comes from Poland. In fact, his grandma and other relatives still live in Israel. That must be why he takes so many trips there! Dan told us that his grandma has had the biggest impact on his life because she gave him confidence and made him feel like he could accomplish anything. Dan loves his family for teaching him everything about being Jewish.

Dan's family belongs to Beth Joseph Synagogue in Denver. They follow some Jewish traditions, but not all of them. They go to the synagogue once a month and try to celebrate Shabbat. Sometimes they invite some of their family over for Shabbat.

According to Dan, it was easier to be more observant when he was younger and wasn't involved in so many activities. But he has made a commitment to his religion and has stuck with it. He's proud that he has become more observant in his Judaism as he has gotten older.

Passover and Hanukkah are Dan's favorite holidays. He and his family go to their synagogue during Jewish holidays. Sometimes in school, Dan has felt left out because kids of other religions get days off to celebrate their holidays, while he has to miss school and make up his work later. Once, in seventh grade, his teacher even made him do his work before he missed school to celebrate a Jewish holiday with his family.

Dan's favorite memory of growing up Jewish was when he had his Bar Mitzvah. His friends and relatives came from all over the United States, Mexico, and Israel to celebrate with him. They were proud of what he had accomplished when they heard him read from the Torah and lead the service. Dan had to study for his Bar Mitzvah for five months! His friends would ask him to play baseball, but because he wanted to study for his Bar Mitzvah, he usually didn't go with them. They didn't understand why he was so committed to studying, but Dan knew how important it was.

Dan is involved in a Jewish youth group called B'nai B'rith Youth Organization (BBYO). This is an organization for Jewish kids all over the world. Dan has met most of his Jewish friends through this youth group. BBYO is involved in lots of things. They have helped Russian families come to America and held food drives.

Dan loves playing basketball, football, and baseball and going to movies with his friends. In the future, he wants to go to the University of California at Los Angeles. His dream is to play basketball in the NBA, but since he doesn't think that will happen, his other goal is to go to law school and become a sports agent.

Dan's hero is his grandfather. His grandpa dresses up in his clown outfit and visits hospitals and other places. Dan wants to be as well-known and well-liked as his grandpa. More than anything, Dan wants everyone to be proud of their her-itage and to reach for the sky. He says that even if you just get halfway, that's good.

GOING THROUGH LIFE

All people start on different paths in life, but we all end up at the same place. The cycle of life keeps us all connected. A life cycle is all about growing up. It's a person's own history. We hope you have enjoyed traveling the road of life with our four friends, learning about Jewish young people, and seeing where your paths of your life cross with theirs.

MUSIC, THEATER, AND DANCE

In this chapter you will find
Jewish music of every kind.
You dance and sing,
Because Jewish music is a special thing.

There are lots of different kinds of Jewish music. There is music for praying and there are songs for celebrations and ceremonies. Music has always been used as an expression of Jewish life. It is used on holidays and at many Jewish festivities, such as weddings and Bar/Bat Mitzvahs. Jewish prayer is almost totally based on music and poetry that come from the heart and soul of the Jewish people.

Ever since Judaism began, there has been song and dance. A lot of the ancient music is still around today. Jews use music to soothe the soul and to make people happy. Even when Jews were being kicked out of different areas, they took their songs and music with them. As they moved to America, they added American rhythms, like jazz and swing, to some of their music.

Jewish music is still passed down from generation to generation and has survived over the years.

RELIGIOUS MUSIC AND THE CANTOR

Religious music is an important part of the Jewish culture. In synagogue, there is a person called the "cantor." One of the cantor's jobs is to be the music leader. We went to the Hebrew Educational Alliance, a Conservative Jewish synagogue, and met Cantor Martin Goldstein.

As cantor, Mr. Goldstein leads the songs during the service in the synagogue. When he sings, he has to reflect the feelings and meanings of the Hebrew prayers.

Cantor Martin Goldstein

If it is a happy prayer, then the music is fast and happy. If it is a sad prayer, then the music is slow and sad.

When we visited Cantor Goldstein, he told us about his life. Both of his parents were musicians and his father was a cantor. In fact, Cantor Goldstein is the seventh generation in his family to be a cantor. When Martin was five or six years old, he started singing all around the country with his mother and father. They gave concerts in English, Hebrew, and Yiddish. Growing up, Martin loved all kinds of music. When he was young, he was in a rock band with his brother, but still loved the Jewish music that he grew up with. He kept kosher and observed the Sabbath and led a regular life.

One of his many jobs is to teach Hebrew school. He teaches kids who are about to celebrate their Bar/Bat Mitzvahs. He attends and helps perform many Jewish events such as weddings and funerals. Another job is to make sure that the synagogue has a musical life. All prayers are chanted or sung, including the reading of the Torah. Each holiday has its own music that goes with the prayers. Some of the melodies are so old that no one knows how old they are.

Cantor Goldstein told us that music is used to teach small children about being Jewish and about the Torah. For example, the song "Shabbat Shalom" is taught to most young Jewish children. This song welcomes the Sabbath and begins teaching about this special day. We learned that even Barney the dinosaur sings the alef-bet, the Hebrew alphabet. This song was written by a wonderful Jewish woman named Debbie Friedman. Hebrew songs aren't just used in religious services. They are heard on TV and worldwide. The song "Hava Negila" (HAH-vah Neh-GEEL-lah) has made its way into American culture, and it is even played at hockey and baseball games.

Cantor Goldstein said, "Music isn't unique to Judaism, because all cultures have it. But the Jewish music is unique." Cantor Goldstein feels that the most important thing he does as a cantor is teach about the music. He believes that if there weren't any music, there would not be any Jewish faith! He even makes tapes to send home with people so they can keep learning at home.

YIDDISH THEATER

In addition to music in the synagogue, music has also been an important part of the Jewish theater. There used to be Yiddish theaters in America in the early 1900s. They performed Shakespearean and other plays in Yiddish. Yiddish was used a lot around the time of World War II. It was so popular because many Jews who had immigrated from Eastern Europe didn't speak English, but they did speak Yiddish. As American Jews became more and more a part of the American culture, they stopped speaking Yiddish as a language. Some Jews still use Yiddish words and phrases today, but Yiddish theaters have seen their final curtain. However, we've written about one of the most famous actresses in the Yiddish theater. Her name is Molly Picon.

Molly Picon

Molly Picon was a famous Yiddish theater performer. We want to tell you a little bit about her life. Molly Picon was born in New York City in 1898. She started in show business when she was very young. At age five, Molly became so famous that she changed her name to Margaret. Ms. Picon even won money for her singing and dancing ability on stage.

In 1918 she went to a Vaudeville act. This was where people sang, danced, and performed comedy acts. Ms. Picon became a major Yiddish star. When the Yiddish theater wasn't as popular as it used to be, she played on Broadway, starring as Becky Felderman in *Morning Star* in 1940. The Congress for Jewish Culture presented Ms. Picon with the first of her ten Goldy Awards in 1985.

JEWISH MUSICIANS

Jewish people are well known for supporting the music and art programs in their communities. They love to attend concerts and shows. But more than just supporting music, there are lots and lots of famous musicians who are Jewish. Cantor Goldstein told us about Kenny G, Al Jolson, Irving Berlin, Itzhak Perlman, George and Ira Gershwin, Neil Diamond, and Barbra

Conductor Leonard Slatkin

Streisand. There are also great conductors who are Jewish. Leonard Slatkin is a conductor and music director for the St. Louis Symphony Orchestra. Leonard Bernstein conducted the New York Philharmonic. There are so many famous Jewish people we could have sat there for a whole year and talked about them all! We would like to share a few of these people with you.

George Gershwin

One of the most famous composers of all times is George Gershwin. He was born in Brooklyn, New York, in 1898.

George lived in a poor Jewish community and heard very little music until he was 12. Then his parents bought him a piano. George quickly taught himself to play and became very good at writing pop-

ular songs, musicals, piano works, and operas. He became one of the country's most gifted composers.

During the 1920s and the 1930s, he wrote many successful musicals and music for films. His brother, Ira Gershwin, wrote words to his songs. Together they were Broadway's most successful musical team. Some of their most famous works are: "Rhapsody in Blue," "Swanee," and the opera *Porgy and Bess.* His songs are still heard today, and his musicals are still performed all over America.

Irving Berlin

Irving Berlin was born on May 11, 1888, in Eastern Russia. His father was a *shochet,* a person who slaughters animals in the Jewish tradition, and he was also a prayer leader in the synagogue. His family left Russia because of all the problems and moved to America.

Mr. Berlin wrote many patriotic popular songs as well as some non-Jewish music. Some of his most famous songs are "Easter Parade," "White Christmas," and "G-d Bless America."

Mr. Berlin supported Jewish charities and donated money to worthwhile causes. On February 18, 1955, President Eisenhower gave Irving Berlin a gold medal in recognition of his services in composing many patriotic songs for America. He is remembered in the Jewish War Veterans Museum in Washington, D.C. He should feel proud of himself because he wrote 900 songs, 19 musicals, and music for 18 movies! He died on September 22, 1984, at the age of 101.

Yehudi Menuhin

Yehudi Menuhin is a world-famous violinist. He was born on April 22, 1916. His parents were both born in Russia, but his father grew up in Palestine. Yehudi was born in New York and was raised in California. His parents were poor and couldn't afford a baby sitter, so young Yehudi went to the concerts with them. This is probably why he started playing the violin at age three. When he was seven years old, he had his first public solo appearance. It wouldn't be his last.

Later in his life, Yehudi Menuhin played with many famous orchestras and conductors. He traveled during World War II and played for American and Allied armed forces. He was the first American to perform in the Soviet Union after the war. He also used his talents to raise money to help the needy. In 1952, he toured India and raised $74,000 to help a famine fund. Yehudi Menuhin is now known around the world. People have called him "America's Best Ambassador" because of his interest in other cultures.

Yehudi Menuhin

Students learn to dance the hora

JEWISH DANCING

Jewish dancing brings Jewish people together and is possibly the best known way to express joy and happiness. It is said that when Moses led the Jewish people out of Egypt, his sister Miriam led the women of the 12 tribes in a victory dance. At Orthodox weddings or other celebrations, Jewish men and women dance separately. Today most other Jews dance together.

During our workshop we had a good time learning Jewish folk dances. Rachel Mor taught us the songs and dance steps. When we interviewed Ms. Mor, we found out a lot more about her. Here are a few things that we found interesting.

Rachel Mor was born July 13, 1953, in Israel. Ms. Mor considers herself an Israeli-American Jew. America is her home today. Ms. Mor has always loved to dance. When she was young and went to dance performances, she would go home and imitate the dances. When she was younger her parents gave her two pine tree seeds to plant. One of the trees died, so she worked hard to protect the other tree. She sang and danced around it. Now her tree is the tallest in the community.

Now Ms. Mor enjoys teaching the dances she learned as a child, especially Jewish and Israeli folk dances. She is a very nice, understanding, artistic person with a very good imagination. We really enjoyed meeting her and learning new dances.

The *hora* is probably the most famous Jewish dance and is danced all over the world. Ms. Mor taught us this dance,

HAVAH NAGILAH

The hora is traditionally danced to "Havah Nagilah"

Teaching Jewish songs

which was brought from Eastern Europe to Palestine many years ago and was danced by people in communities in Israel. It is danced now at many happy occasions all across America.

The hora has six basic steps that keep repeating, and it is danced by people holding hands in a circle. You and your friends can learn this dance by following the directions below.

1. Step right with your right foot.
2. Place your left foot directly behind your right foot.
3. Step right with your right foot.
4. Hop on your right foot.
5. Step left with your left foot.
6. Hop on your left foot.

JEWISH SONGS

During our workshop we learned many Jewish songs. Some of us already knew them, but some kids had never heard them before. We had fun teaching and helping each other with the words. We thought that since music is such a big part of being Jewish, we had to have some songs in our book. We got permission to print these songs because the Jewish Kids Catalog was nice and lent them to us.

"Hinei Mah Tovh"

The "Hinei Mah Tovh" (he-NAH ma TOV) is a happy song that is sung in a round. When the first group gets to the second verse, the second group starts singing. The song is about how nice it is when brothers and sisters live together in the same house.

"Shabbat Shalom"

This song celebrates and welcomes the Sabbath, the weekly day of rest. It's an easy song to sing, with two main words, "Bim, bam." The words *Shabbat shalom* mean "have a peaceful Sabbath."

"Havah Nagilah"

This song is very popular in America because it is a traditional song that seems to be sung everywhere. It tells people to have happy hearts. It's often sung at weddings and other happy occasions.

MUSICAL INSTRUMENT

Gragger

A gragger is a musical instrument used at Purim, one of the holidays that we tell you about in the Holidays chapter. It's a noise-maker that you shake whenever Haman's name is mentioned. Haman was the king's evil advisor, who tried to kill all of the Jews of Persia. You can also use the gragger to help keep the rhythm to the songs that we taught you in this chapter. To make a gragger of your own, follow the instructions below.

Materials:
> An empty soda can
> Birdseed, gravel, or anything else that will make noise
> Scissors
> Glue
> Markers, sequins, or any other things you want to decorate your gragger
> Construction paper

Directions:
1. Measure and cut the construction paper so it is the same size as the can.

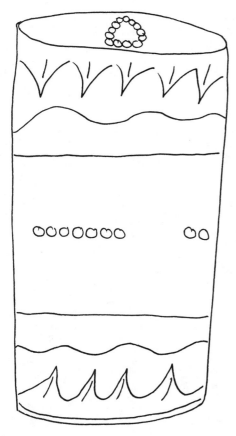

A gragger

2. Decorate one side of the construction paper. Don't glue decorations on until you have the paper on the can.

3. Fill the can with something that will make noise.

4. Put tape over the hole where you would normally drink.

5. Wrap and glue the construction paper around the can and then glue the two ends of the paper together. Decorate.

In this chapter, we could tell you only a little about the way Jewish music was and is today. Jewish people have been involved with the theater and arts for centuries. Without this support, Jewish artists never would have survived through the years. Even today, Jewish people support different kinds of music and arts in America, helping them survive for future generations to enjoy.

Students participate in Jewish dancing

HOLIDAYS AND FESTIVALS

Come with us and celebrate
Our many holidays,
From Purim to Yom Kippur,
We observe in many ways.
On Yom Kippur we fast.
On the Shabbat we all feast.
On Sukkot we shake the lulav,
North, South, West, and East.
On Purim we all dress up
And play silly games.
On Hanukkah we light the candles,
Nine small burning flames.
Shavuot comes in early summer,
Yom Ha'Atzma'ut in the spring.
Rosh Hashana is the new year,
Resolutions it will bring.

In this chapter, we explore many Jewish holidays. They each have special traditions, and people eat different kinds of foods. Even though there are many different holidays, they all have something to do with the Torah—the Jewish Bible—and they all start at sunset. The best part of holidays is that you get to spend time with your family and sometimes you get to have your friends over. We hope you enjoy reading about holidays.

HEBREW CALENDAR

You may have noticed that some of your friends might celebrate Hanukkah in late November or December. The Jewish holidays follow the Hebrew calendar and will only fall on the same American calendar date every 19 years.

The Hebrew calendar is 11 days shorter than the general calendar because it is based on the cycle of the moon. The

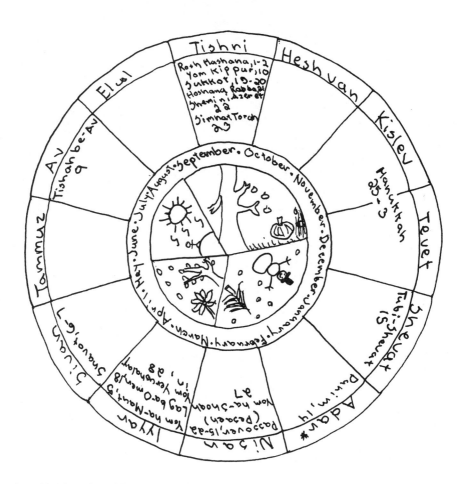

The months and holidays of the Hebrew calendar

moon circles the earth 12 times in 354 days, one year on the Hebrew calendar. The beginning of each rotation the moon makes is the beginning of a new month. The Hebrew calendar started 3,760 years before the common calendar started. It starts with the beginning of the earth as it's told in the Bible.

First, we want to explain about the very special day called Shabbat, which is celebrated once each week. Pretty neat, huh? A holiday every week!

SHABBAT

Jewish families across America celebrate Shabbat—their word for Sabbath or day of rest—in many different ways. We are going to talk about the traditional Jewish ways of celebrating Shabbat.

In the beginning, according to the Book of Genesis, G-d said, "There will be seven days in the week. Six days will be for work and the seventh will be for rest." Shabbat starts every Friday just before sunset and ends on Saturday when there are at least three stars in the sky.

Shabbat starts when the mother of the house lights candles and says a special blessing. She usually covers her head to show her respect for G-d. She also sings songs. When it is time to eat, the man of the house leads the *kiddush* (kid-OOSH), a blessing over the wine. Then someone says *hamotzi* (ha-MOAT-ze), the blessing over the *challah* (HA-lah) or bread. Challah is an egg bread made with six braids of dough and it is shared by everyone. The reason it has six braids is to remind people that six days out of the week you should work and you should rest on the seventh day. Some families will eat off good plates that they don't use the rest of the week. Shabbat is also a time to gather with family and friends. After the service at home, some families go to the synagogue.

On Saturday mornings, the first thing some Jewish people do is go to the synagogue to pray and study the Torah. People can spend three or four hours praying in the synagogue. Some Jews walk to the synagogue and do not use a car.

It is important that Jewish people rest during Shabbat. They are not supposed to work at all. We think working might be lifting heavy things or doing hard stuff, but "work" can also mean things like using a pen or pencil, talking on the phone, driving a car, turning on the TV, using money, or starting a fire for cooking. Some Jewish people will turn on a few lights before Shabbat starts and leave them on all night. They might also keep their ovens on all night long at a low temperature. Turn-

The Torah scroll wrapped in a decorated cloth

ing things on and off is considered "work." When Jewish people say that they are supposed to rest during Shabbat, they mean it.

The ending of Shabbat is called *Havdalah* (hav-DAH-lah), which means "separation" in Hebrew. During Havdalah there are special prayers you do to show that Shabbat is different from the rest of the week. We made three things to learn about Havdalah. We made a Havdalah candle out of beeswax. Then we got to make a special spice box and filled it with cloves that smelled good. The spices are used during the Havdalah service to remember the sweetness of Shabbat. We also decorated a plastic wine cup to look like a kiddush cup. The candle is put out in the wine to remind us that Shabbat is over and it is time to go back to work. Find out

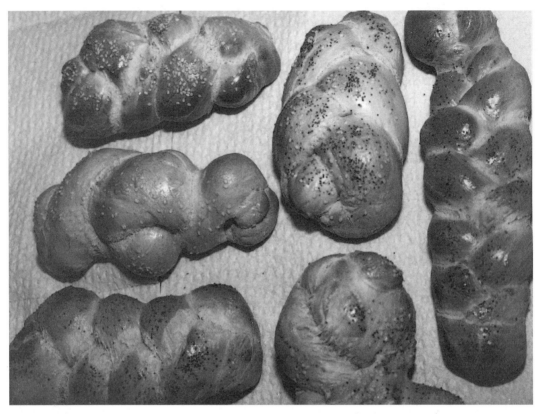

Challah bread

more about these crafts in the Hands-on Fun chapter of this book.

ROSH HASHANA

If you have any Jewish friends, you may want to say *"L'Shanah Tova Tikotevu* (leh-shah-NAH toh-VAH tee-kah-TEH-voo)"* to wish them a happy new year. But you wouldn't say that in January, you would say it usually in September. For Jews, the new year is called Rosh Hashana (ROSH ha-SHAH-nah). Many Jewish kids are absent from school to go to their syna-gogue to celebrate and pray for a good new year. During their prayers, they think about good deeds they want to do in the upcoming year.

Jewish people have an interesting way to announce the new year. Many centuries ago, a great horn called a *shofar* (show-FAHR) was blown to let the Jews know it was a new year. This is still done today. The shofar is a ram's horn. It is blown more than 100 times on Rosh Hashana.

The first ten days of the seventh month on the Jewish calendar are called the High Holidays. Some Jews call this time *Yamim Noraim* (yah-MEEM no-rah-EEM), which means "the day of judgment." Many Jews around the world believe that there is a Book of Life, where people's deeds are recorded. On Rosh Hashana, Jews believe that G-d begins to watch people's actions very closely. During the Jewish High Holidays, G-d's holy book is kept open. As the sun goes down on *Yom Kippur* (yohm kee-POOR), the tenth day of Tishri, G-d writes down what their life will be like in the coming year.

A widely practiced custom is for Jewish people to go to a river on the first afternoon of Rosh Hashana, turn their pockets inside out, and shake all their sins into the water. Then they recite prayers to apologize for all the bad things they have done in the past year. The river washes the sins clean or carries them far away. Some people today save their bread crumbs from Shabbat and throw them to the fish or the ducks when they go to the river.

Something nice to do during Rosh Hashana is to send cards and sweets to Jewish people to let them know you are thinking about themduring this special time. If you're lucky, they might invite you to share some of the delicious foods they eat for Rosh Hashana! Traditionally, Jewish people eat apples dipped in honey on Rosh Hashana to help bring in a sweet year. They may also dip torn pieces of challah into the honey. The challah for Rosh Hashana is special because it is round and sometimes has raisins in it to symbolize a full and sweet year. Honey cake is a very popular dessert for Rosh Hashana. It is fun to bake. It tastes sweet and cinnamony. You will find the recipe in the Hands-on Fun chapter.

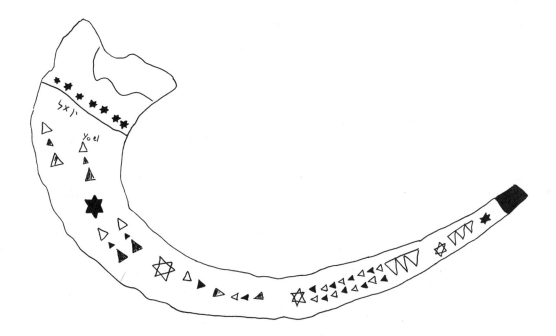

A student making a craft

YOM KIPPUR

Yom Kippur is a very special holiday because it is the Day of Atonement. That's when Jewish people try to make sure they get in the Book of Life for the coming year. They usually go to synagogue and pray all day. They ask G-d to forgive all the bad things they have done. They ask the people they have hurt for forgiveness. Yom Kippur is a time to make your enemies into your friends and to learn how to forgive.

Some Jews wear white to synagogue because white stands for purity. The white robes that the men wear are called *kittels*. Some don't wear leather to show respect for the lives of animals.

Another way some Jews show G-d that they want forgiveness is by going without food or water from sundown to sunset the next day. Fasting shows G-d that they are really serious about asking for forgiveness. Pregnant women, kids under 13, and people who are ill are excused from fasting. Not eating and drinking for a whole day is hard to do!

The very first prayer of Yom Kippur is *Kol Nidre* (kol NEE-dray), which means "all vows." It releases everyone from vows made during the year. It is a long, beautiful song, which is repeated three times to make sure G-d hears it. On the afternoon of Yom Kippur, the Bible story of "Jonah and the Whale" is read in the synagogue. The story of Jonah reminds the Jews that G-d knows what everyone is doing. As the sun goes down, the *Neilah* (nah-ee-LAH) prayer is sung. Then there is one last and very long blast on the shofar, and Yom Kippur is over.

SUKKOT

Sukkot (su-KOAT) is the celebration of the harvest. It usually falls in the month of October. Sukkot lasts eight days. Some Jewish people will build *sukkahs* (su-KAHS), or huts, in their backyards. The sukkah has at least three sides and the top is open a little so you can see the stars. The roof is made from something natural that grows from the ground, such as the branches from a tree. It looks like a little tree house on the ground. The sukkah represents the temporary homes Jews lived in when they were wandering in the desert for 40 years, or the shelters used by the farmers during the harvest time. Some families eat their meals in the sukkah and some people even sleep in them. Sukkahs are sometimes decorated with fruits and vegetables that represent the harvest.

There are two more symbols that are used to celebrate the holiday of Sukkot. The *etrog* (ET-rog) is one of these symbols. An etrog is a citrus fruit that looks like a bumpy lemon and smells wonderful! The other symbol is the *lulav* (LOO-lav). The lulav is a bundle of branches from three separate trees. On the first and last days of Sukkot people go to synagogues and pray. They recite *hallel* (ha-LELL), which are psalms of praise that are sung on special holidays. On the last day of Sukkot, Jews pray for rain for the new crops.

Authors sit in the sukkah they built

SIMCHAT TORAH

Simchat Torah (sim-KHAT toe-RAH) follows the holiday of Sukkot. It is the holiday that celebrates having finished reading the whole Torah in a year. On this day the very last section of the Torah is read, and then the Torah is scrolled back to the beginning to start reading all over again.

Simchat Torah is celebrated by going to the synagogue and dancing, singing, waving the flag of Israel, and parading the Torah around the synagogue. During Simchat Torah, some synagogues have a special ceremony that welcomes the youngest children into the congregation. Then they can begin their religious schooling. Each child is given a small paper Torah to be reminded of this special day.

HANUKKAH

Hanukkah (HAH-nuh-kah) is a Jewish holiday that usually takes place in December. It is very popular in America today. Hanukkah, which means "dedication" in Hebrew, is also known as the "Festival of Lights." Jews rededicate themselves to their Judaism and to G-d on Hanukkah.

Hanukkah is a celebration of freedom. More than 2,000 years ago, the land of Israel was ruled by the Greeks. Their evil king, Antiochus, tried to force the Jews to give up their beliefs and worship Greek idols. Judah Maccabees and his followers fought back until the Greeks gave up. On the first Hanukkah, the Maccabees rededicated the temple in Jerusalem to G-d. They

had only enough oil left in the *menorah* (meh-NOR-ah)—called the *Hanukiyah* (han-u-KEY-ah)—to last for one day, but it miraculously lasted for eight days. This is why Hanukkah is celebrated for eight days.

During the Hanukkah celebration, many Jewish people get together with family members and say special blessings. They often light several menorahs so that everyone can have their own. When all of the menorahs are lit, it is a beautiful sight.

Potato *latkes* (LOT-kahs) are fried potato pancakes that you can eat with applesauce or sour cream. Some Jewish people also like to eat jelly doughnuts during this time. Both of these foods are cooked in oil, reminding Jews of the oil that lasted so long in the temple. Some Jewish children like to play with the *dreidel* (DRAY-duhl and exchange presents for Hanukkah.

Hanukkah is a very fun time. Lots of Jewish kids wait for this celebration all year long, the way Christian kids wait for

Christmas. You can find out how to make a menorah, cook potato latkes, and play a game with a dreidel in the Hands-on Fun chapter of this book.

PURIM

Purim (POO-rem) is the holiday that usually falls in March. Purim is a joyful celebration of Queen Esther's bravery against the evil Haman. During the Purim celebration, Jews put on plays, give gifts, and have carnivals. People also dress in masks and costumes. It is like a Jewish Halloween. In our workshop, we made traditional Purim cookies called *Hamantashen*. These tasty cookies are shaped like Haman's triangular hat. You can find out how to make them in the Hands-on Fun chapter. Some Jews give baskets that are filled with Hamantashen, fruits, and candies. They also give money to help the poor.

On Purim it is traditional to shout "boos" and shake graggers, which are noisemakers, whenever Haman's name is mentioned. Get ready to boo as we tell you the *megillah* (mah-GEEL-ah), or story, of Esther.

Once there was a king named Ahasuerus. King Ahasuerus got so angry with his queen that he had her killed. When the king decided to choose a new queen, he told his adviser Haman to send for all the young women in his kingdom.

Esther, a young Jewish orphan, was taken away from her cousin Mordecai to appear in front of the king. The king chose Esther to be the queen. Mordecai was a wise Jewish nobleman. One day, he heard two guards planning to kill the king. Mordecai informed Esther. Esther told the king and the guards were punished. Mordecai and Queen Esther had saved the king's life!

One day the evil and the powerful Haman was passing through the king's gate. Everyone bowed before him, but Mordecai would not.

"Who are you?" said Haman angrily. "How dare you stand when you know that all must bow to me!"

"My name is Mordecai," said the man. "I will not bow to you. I must not bow to anyone except G-d. I am a Jew."

Haman was filled with anger. Haman said to himself, "I will kill all the Jews."

Mordecai told Esther that she must plead with the king for her people. "I may not go to the king unless he summons me," she said.

"If you don't go, all the Jews in the land will die," he said.

"You are right," admitted Esther, and she went to see the king.

A student making Hamantashen cookies

The king wondered why Esther came to him even though he had not summoned her. But he loved Esther and he gave her permission to speak with him. Esther asked him to grant her one wish and, of course, the king said that he would. She told the king about Haman's evil plan to kill all of the Jews in the kingdom. Esther revealed that she was a Jew and also the cousin of Mordecai, who had saved the king's life. She begged the king to save the Jews from Haman's threat of death. The king told Esther that he couldn't take back the order that Haman had made, but that he would allow the Jews to take up their weapons and defend themselves.

So on the 13th day of Adar, Haman and his sons were hanged, and the Jews defeated those who had planned to kill them. Mordecai said that the Jews should celebrate on the 14th day of Adar from then on, and they named that day Purim.

PASSOVER

Passover is one of the most important holidays for Jewish people. It's a celebration to help them remember how the Israelites were finally freed from slavery in Egypt. Here's the Passover story as we've retold it from the Bible.

Long ago, a small group of Hebrew people came to Egypt because there was not enough food in their land. The pharaoh of Egypt gave the Israelites good land and let them live however they wanted. Later, an evil pharaoh took over the land. He made the Israelites his slaves and forced them to build Egyptian cities.

One day G-d spoke to Moses through a burning bush, telling him to go to the pharaoh and tell him to let His people go from Egypt. Moses did this, but the pharaoh said no.

So G-d sent ten plagues to Egypt. First, he made the water into blood. Then he sent lots of frogs, lice, wild beasts, cattle sickness, body sores, hail, locusts, and caused darkness to throughout the land.

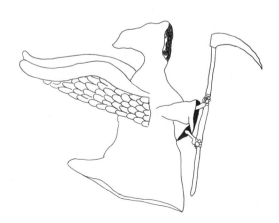

Then G-d spoke to Moses again and said that He would send the most terrible plague of all to Egypt. Moses went to the people of Israel and told them what to do to protect themselves from this last plague. "This night the Angel of Death will pass over all the land. He shall kill the first born son of each family. Even the pharaoh's son will die. Sacrifice a lamb and spread some of its blood on the doorposts of your houses. If you do this, death will pass over your home."

On Passover, the Egyptians lost all their first-born sons, but the first-born sons of the Israelites lived. The pharaoh was terrified. He ordered all the Israelites to leave Egypt at once, and Moses led his people out of Egypt.

Later, though, the pharaoh decided he still needed the Israelites as slaves. He ordered his soldiers to find them and bring them back to Egypt as prisoners. The Israelites were scared when they realized the Egyptian army was coming after them. They were trapped, with the Red Sea on one side and the army on the other. They asked G-d for help. So G-d parted the Red Sea for them. As the Israelites crossed the sea with the Egyptians chasing them, the Red Sea closed behind them and the Egyptian army drowned.

Today in America, Passover is celebrated for eight days. A special meal called a *Seder* (SAY-der) is prepared and eaten during the first two evenings of Passover. The night before the Seder, everything has to be ready. For this special holiday meal, most families have special dishes that are used only for Passover.

If you went to a Jewish family's Seder, you would learn about the Passover from a book called the *Haggadah* (ha-GAH-dah). This book was written so that everyone could understand the story of the Passover.

During the Seder a special order is followed. The word *seder* means "order." First, an adult says the kiddush blessing over a glass of wine to remember the fruits of the earth. A special plate called the "Seder plate" has symbols on it as a reminder of the hard times the Jewish people experienced during the time of slavery in Egypt. Jews eat a bitter herb like horseradish to remember the bitterness of slavery in Egypt. They eat charoset, which is a crumbly, cinnamony mixture of apples, nuts, and wine, to remind them of the mortar between the bricks they used in building the cities for the pharaoh when they were slaves. When they taste it now, they remember how sweet it is to be free. Parsley is dipped in the salt water as a reminder of the tears shed when the Jews were slaves. Another symbol is the shank bone of a lamb. It is a reminder of the lamb the Jews ate at the first Passover. The last symbol is the egg. It represents the birth of a new year and is a symbol of life.

The *matzo* (MAHT-sah) cracker is an important part of the Seder dinner. When the pharaoh let the Jews go, they didn't have time to let the bread rise. It was hard and flat. Now, the Jewish people eat matzo every year instead of regular bread, to remember that the Jews were in a hurry to leave Egypt. Before the Seder meal, a piece of matzo is broken and half is hidden by an adult. Everyone then eats dinner. After

An author makes a Seder plate

dinner, the children go and look for the hidden matzo, called *afikomen* (ah-fee-KO-men). This is a fun part of the ceremony because the finder gets a prize. When the matzo is found by the children, everyone shares a bit of it. This reminds Jewish people that long ago there were special gifts brought to the temple in Jerusalem and shared with everyone.

Another custom during the Passover ceremony is to put out a cup to welcome Elijah. Elijah was a wise prophet and a very important teacher who lived around 800 B.C.E. Before he died, Elijah said that he would return once each generation, disguised as a poor person, and visit people's homes to see how they would treat him. The cup is filled with wine during the

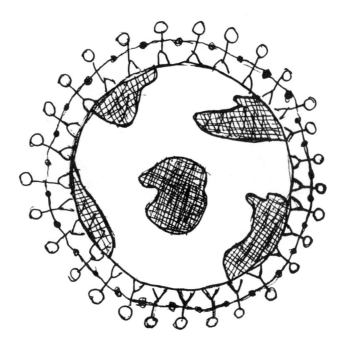

Seder dinner. At the end of the meal, the cup is checked to see if Elijah has visited. Believe us—Elijah always comes and drinks some of the wine at everybody's Seder!

If you are ever invited to a Seder, be sure to go. We thought it was a really neat and meaningful experience—and lots of fun, too!

YOM HA'ATZMA'UT

Not long ago, many Jews had a wish that their children and their grandchildren could live in a land they could call their own. On May 14, 1948, that wish came true. Israel became its own nation. It was a happy time because many countries had kicked the Jews out. After 2,000 years of struggling, the homeland of the Jews had finally been restored. Today Jewish Ameri-cans remember Israel's independence with a giant celebration called *Yom Ha'Atzma'ut* (yohm ha-AHTS-mah-oot), which usually falls during May. The sounds of whistles, cheering, and laughing can be heard during this exciting and festive holiday.

Some communities have very large carnivals or picnics in synagogues or community centers. Many Jews like to eat traditional Israeli food at the celebration, such as *falafel* (fah-LAH-fel) in pita bread. Both of these foods together make something that looks like a Jewish taco, and they're delicious! Many Jews also celebrate by dancing the hora, which is an Israeli dance. When you think about Yom Ha'Atzma'ut, think the Fourth of July! The two holidays are very similar. If you want, you can find out how to dance the hora earlier in the Music, Theater, and Dance chapter.

SHAVUOT

Shavuot (shah-voo-OHT) is a holiday celebrating the gift of the Torah. Tradition tells us that G-d spoke to Moses on Mt. Sinai and gave him the Torah written on stone tablets. Shavuot means "weeks" in Hebrew, and it comes exactly seven weeks after Passover.

In America, Shavuot lasts for two days. Some Jews will stay up all night studying the Torah. A scribe writes the Torah, which usually takes two years to make it perfect. The congregation is very excited when a new Torah is bought. The synagogue sometimes has a special ceremony to dedicate the Torah on Shavuot. If a Torah contains any mistakes or is damaged, it cannot just be thrown away. The rabbi will bury it in the ground, to show respect for G-d and His name. Actually, anything that has the name of G-d must be buried in this special way.

TISHAH B'AV

Tishah B'Av (TEESH-uh BOV) is a day of mourning and sadness. It means the "Ninth of Av," the Hebrew month that falls during July or August. On this day, adults don't eat or drink anything from sundown to sundown in order to remember what happened long ago.

The Holy Temple in Jerusalem was destroyed on Tishah B'Av in 586 B.C.E. The second Temple was destroyed 656 years later on the same day. The Jews were

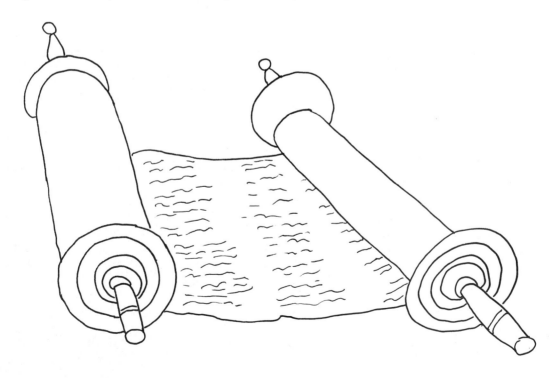

sent into exile and wandered the world for 2,000 years until the founding of Israel.

The Temples meant a lot to the Jews. Jews remember the sadness over the loss of their temples on Tishah B'Av. They also remember when they weren't free to practice their religion without being criticized or getting thrown out of some country.

Jews around the world light mourning candles in the evening of Tishah B'Av. Some wear uncomfortable shoes or take them off and sit on hard benches or on the floor during the services. They want G-d to know that they are being respectful, not thinking of themselves and their own comfort. Rabbis call this day a day of misfortune or "The Dark Fast" because of the sadness caused by the destruction of the Holy Temples. But many Jews also believe that the Messiah will come to Earth on Tishah B'Av. Jews often think about this so they will not be too sad.

Jewish holidays are full of wonderful things to do and learn. You can find holiday recipes, games, and crafts in the Hands-On Fun chapter of this book. Sharing the fun is the best part.

FAMOUS FIRSTS AND HEROES

Albert Einstein was a Jew.
What do you know?—Houdini was, too.
So was Isaac Mayer Wise
And Steven Spielberg . . . what a surprise!
These people have done many great things,
From making movies to escaping from rings.
As you read this chapter you will learn
How these people helped the world turn.

Our lives have been affected by the contributions that many Jewish Americans have made to our country. Jewish Americans play an important role in shaping America's history. Every day our lives are touched by music, books, medicine, science, movies, TV, religion, and politics. Jewish Americans are actively involved in each of these areas.

It was difficult to decide which Jews to highlight for our book. Many of our biographies were based on our own interests, as well as the leadership roles and accomplishments of our subjects. We chose some individuals because of their commitment to *tzedakah* (tsah-dah-KAH), which means giving to those who are in need. The famous Jews we selected gave back to their community in some way.

After you read this chapter, we hope you'll understand more about what Jewish Americans have done for this country and who they are on the inside. Some suffered in their countries of birth and wanted a better life for themselves and their families. Others were born here and have held on to their Jewish heritage, whether they play baseball, compose music, travel in space, make judicial decisions, or act in movies.

FEATURED BIOGRAPHIES

Harry Houdini (1847–1926)

Who is that man in the straitjacket being lowered into the river? It's Harry Houdini!

Harry Houdini was a famous magician, whose real name was Ehrich Weiss.

Harry Houdini

He was born on March 24, 1874, in Budapest, Hungary, a poor city in eastern Europe. Ehrich's father, Samuel Weiss, was a rabbi who led a small Jewish congregation. His dad was offered a job in America as a rabbi in Wisconsin. They had heard that America was the land of opportunity, so they decided to move.

At age nine, Ehrich amazed his friends with the tricks he performed. One of his childhood tricks was for someone to tie a rope around his hands, then he would undo the knots and escape. When he grew up and went to high school, he became a strong athlete, which helped him as he performed. After high school, Weiss became interested in Robert Houdin, a French magician. Wanting to follow in the footsteps of Houdin, he changed his name

to Houdini. He practiced more and more daring tricks. He handcuffed himself to poles and then practiced getting out of them. He tried to learn everything about locks so he could be an expert.

Houdini and one of his brothers began doing magic shows in a museum, but they weren't successful. At the museum, Harry met a singer named Bess Rahner, and they married. The Houdini Brothers broke up, and Harry and Bess went into business together. Bess had no experience, but she quickly learned her part in the act.

Harry's big break came when British police announced that they had handcuffs that couldn't be opened without a key. Harry asked the police to handcuff him and attach him to a pole. The media and police watched. They were about to leave for an hour, but before they could Mr. Houdini asked, "Don't you want your handcuffs back?" By the time everyone turned around to answer, he had already removed them. Everyone was astounded!

In future years, Mr. Houdini would escape from jail cells, straitjackets, closed coffins, and many other dangerous situations. During one of his shows, though, he dared an audience member to punch him in the stomach. He was caught by surprise and the blow was fatal. Harry Houdini will be remembered as one of the greatest magicians of all time.

Emma Lazarus (1849–1887)

"Give me your tired, your poor, your huddled masses . . . " Do you know where this famous quotation comes from and who wrote it? It was written by Emma Lazarus and is carved on the Statue of Liberty in New York City.

Ms. Lazarus was born on July 22, 1849. Her parents were wealthy Jews devoted to their family. Young Emma was privately tutored and curious about everything. When she was a teenager, she had a book of poems published called *Poems and Translations.* A famous writer of the time, Ralph Waldo Emerson, liked her poems. Mr. Emerson invited Emma to spend a week at his house in Massachusetts. They were friends for the rest of their lives.

In the late 1870s, Ms. Lazarus was asked to translate and write a prayer book. Ms. Lazarus did not like "Jewish things" until she found out how poorly Russian Jews were being treated. She was disgusted at the cruelty and unfair treatment of Jews in Russia. Her writing dealt with her feelings towards the Jewish community. Ms. Lazarus dreamt of the Jewish people having a homeland of their own. She continued to work for fair treatment of Jews. Ms. Lazarus used her own money so that people could come to America from Europe.

Ms. Lazarus will be remembered for her contributions to America and her inscription on the Statue of Liberty.

Albert Einstein (1879–1955)

What do you get when you cross a head of fuzzy white hair and a bunch of scientific formulas? You get Albert Einstein—one of the greatest scientists who ever lived.

Albert Einstein was born on March 14, 1879, in Ulm, Germany. Albert was the only Jewish child in his class and lots of kids teased him. Even back then he had his own theory—socks were a waste of time. So he never wore socks.

When Mr. Einstein was young, he thought school was dull and unimaginative. His teachers thought that Albert would never be a good student. They considered him slow because he had a hard time speaking. When Albert was 16, he tried to get into college, but failed the entrance exam. But he always liked to study math and science on his own. So he studied hard and one year later he passed it. He studied science and math at The Federal Institute of Technology in Zurich, Switzerland.

Mr. Einstein was asked to be in the German army, but he refused to join because he never wanted to wear a German uniform. He didn't agree with the government in Germany. He didn't even believe in

war, and he didn't like the German government telling people how they should live their lives. When he was visiting America in 1933, the Nazis raided Mr. Einstein's house in Germany. He decided to stay in the United States. Since then, his ideas have given people a new understanding about time, space, gravity, and the nature of light. He was never caught by the Germans and became a United States citizen in 1940. In America, he kept studying and met with President Franklin Roosevelt to talk about the atomic bomb. He also helped invent a new kind of refrigerator and a camera.

Albert Einstein believed in many causes. He believed in Zionism. A Zionist is a person who strongly believes that there should be a Jewish country. Mr. Einstein was even offered the job as President of Israel, but he turned it down. Another cause Mr. Einstein believed in was world peace. Mr. Einstein didn't like people hurting one another.

Albert Einstein died in Princeton, New Jersey, on April 18, 1955, but his ideas about physics are still being taught today to millions of students in classrooms all over the world.

Ann Landers (b. 1918)

Esther Pauline Friedman was born on July 4, 1918, in Sioux City, Iowa. She has three sisters, and one of them is her twin. When she was born, her parents named her Esther Pauline Friedman and her twin sister, Pauline Esther.

Esther Friedman went to Morningside College from 1936 to 1939. When

Ann Landers

the original Ann Landers died, the *Chicago Sun Times* ran a contest to find someone to continue to write the advice column. Esther Pauline was the winner of the contest and became the "new" Ann Landers. In 1955, Ms. Landers began writing her column, "Ask Ann Landers." She received thousands of letters and her sister offered to help her answer the boxes and boxes of letters. Today, Ann Landers' column is printed in over 1,200 newspapers. Her column has nearly 90 million readers.

When Ms. Landers first began her column, she became more aware of problems in America. "I really care about what happens to people, and when I first began to read those letters, it was a real eye-opener," she said. "I came from a very solid Midwestern Jewish home. I led a very sheltered life. I had never seen a man hit his wife. I had never seen drunkenness.

I had never seen any poverty. I knew these things were happening, but they never happened to me. The mail grew me up in a hurry."

Ann Landers is well respected for her advice about life's challenging problems.

Elie Wiesel (b. 1928)

The Holocaust was a time when an evil man named Adolf Hitler and his army rounded up millions of Jews and other people he thought weren't as good as he was and killed them. Six million Jews were massacred in concentration camps. One of the people who survived the camps was a man named Elie Wiesel.

Mr. Wiesel promised himself and others that if he escaped, he would tell the story of the Holocaust to those who didn't know about it and especially to those who had tried to forget or say it never happened. He not only helped Jews, Mr. Wiesel also tried to restore peace and human rights wherever there were problems or people who needed help. He has talked to everyone from groups of children to world leaders. He won the Nobel Peace Prize in 1986 and a Congressional Gold Medal from President Ronald Reagan.

Mr. Wiesel has written some very famous things. Here is one of them:

"I am convinced that one day the dead themselves will speak . . . perhaps they will speak through us. But one day they will speak and on that day the Earth will tremble."

When asked why he helps other races, Mr. Wiesel answered, "Because I have seen what I have seen—that is why I do what I

do." He urged President Bill Clinton to try to end the suffering in Bosnia.

Even as a child, Mr. Wiesel was a good writer. After the Holocaust, he wrote two books. One was titled *Night*. This is his personal account of the Holocaust. Mr. Wiesel is the person who first described

the killings as the "Holocaust." Here is a famous passage from *Night*:

"Never shall I forget that night, the first night in camp, which has turned my life into one long night, seven times cursed and seven times sealed. Never shall I forget that smoke. Never shall I forget those flames that consumed my faith forever. Never shall I forget that nocturnal silence which deprived me for all eternity of the desire to live. Never shall I forget those moments that murdered my G-d and my soul and turned my dreams to dust. Never shall I forget these things, even if I am condemned to live as long as G-d Himself. Never."

Mr. Wiesel's writing helps us to remember and learn from the mistakes of the past, so that we can look forward to a better future.

Sandy Koufax (b. 1935)

Are you a baseball fan? If you are, you'll like Sanford "Sandy" Koufax, also known as "the man with the golden arm." He was one of the greatest baseball pitchers who ever lived.

Sandy Koufax was born in Brooklyn, New York, on December 30, 1935. When he was three years old, his parents divorced. When he was nine, his mother married Irving Koufax. Sandy's favorite sport back then wasn't just baseball. He also liked basketball. He played baseball and basketball when he went to Lafayette High School. His stepfather supported Sandy's baseball and basketball interests. When he graduated from high school in 1952, Sandy received basketball and base-

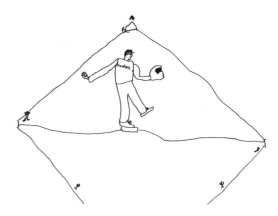

ball scholarships to the University of Cincinnati. He decided to play baseball.

In 1954, Sandy signed with the Brooklyn Dodgers and played with them for 11 years. In 1972, he became the youngest member ever elected to the Baseball Hall of Fame.

In the 1965 World Series, Koufax refused to pitch on Yom Kippur, one of the Jewish High Holidays. The team respected his beliefs and didn't try to force him to play. The team lost that game, but went on to win the World Series. Though he received lots of criticism from the press, Koufax insisted that his personal beliefs were more important than his career.

"Pitching is an art in that the driving force is the pride you have in yourself," Sandy Koufax once said. "I only want to be successful and make my family proud of me."

Steven Spielberg (b. 1947)

Have you ever seen *E.T.* or *Jurassic Park?* If you have, then you know Steven Spielberg. Ever since he was a child, Mr. Spielberg thought about making movies. He is a film

director who has directed films about pirates, aliens, lost arks, dinosaurs, and sharks. But he also has made movies about real life, such as *The Color Purple* and *Schindler's List*.

Steven Spielberg was born on December 18, 1947, in Cincinnati, Ohio. When he was 13, he created his first movie. After he graduated from California State College at Long Beach, Mr. Spielberg directed the science fiction thriller *Close Encounters of the Third Kind*. This movie made a lot of money and set an example for film directors to follow. Some other movies he directed later were *Back to the Future*, *Raiders of the Lost Ark*, *Jaws*, *E.T.*, and *Jurassic Park*.

In 1994, Mr. Spielberg decided to tell the true story of Oscar Schindler, a German businessman who saved more than a thousand Jews from being killed in the Polish concentration camps during World War II. The movie *Schindler's List* is about the Holocaust. Some people who are Holocaust survivors say the film is very realistic. It won an Oscar for Best Picture.

Mr. Spielberg has started a new project called *Survivors of the Shoah*. *Shoah* is the Hebrew word for Holocaust. Mr. Spielberg is interviewing Holocaust survivors to tell the story about what happened to them during World War II. He wants to record the history of more than 75,000 survivors so their stories will never be lost. Mr. Spielberg is paying for the filming of *Survivors of the Shoah* himself.

After the release of *Schindler's List*, he gave copies of that movie to teachers all over the United States for free, to help teach other people about the Holocaust. He is a great filmmaker, but more importantly, he is proud of his Jewish heritage.

Judith Resnick (1949–1986)

Do you like learning about space? Here is a story about one of the first women to become an astronaut.

Judith Resnick was born April 5, 1949, in Cleveland, Ohio. She attended religious school and had a Bat Mitzvah. Ms. Resnick had very good math skills. She earned a perfect score on both her verbal and math SAT's (Scholastic Aptitude Test). Because of Ms. Resnick's high math and science skills, many colleges wanted her to go to their school. Ms. Resnick attended Carnegie-Mellon University in Pittsburgh and received her degree in electrical engineering in 1970. In 1977, Ms. Resnick received her doctorate from the University of Maryland.

Ms. Resnick's life was dedicated to learning about space. She said she was doing what she loved. In 1984, she went into space for the first time. Aboard the first flight on the space shuttle *Discovery*, she served as the mission specialist. She operated the spacecraft's remote-control arm and performed solar-power experiments with a 102-foot-high solar power sail. Her most important mission was to take pictures of Halley's Comet.

When she became an astronaut, Jewish scholars decided she didn't have to celebrate the Sabbath or Jewish holidays in space, because in space it is hard to tell the difference between night and day.

On January 28, 1986, Ms. Resnick boarded the space shuttle *Challenger* with six other crew members. As the shuttle rocketed towards space, it exploded, killing everyone on board. Ms. Resnick will always be remembered as a Jewish woman who died for her country. She is an example to us always to set our goals high and strive to be our best.

Ben Cohen and Jerry Greenfield (b. 1951)

On a hot summer day, when a cold drink won't do, don't you feel like something new? How about a taste of Chunky Monkey ice cream? Or how about some Rain

Forest Crunch? Sound crazy? Maybe—but it's so delicious!

Ben Cohen and Jerry Greenfield were born within a few days of each other in March of 1951, on Long Island, New York. In high school, Ben sold ice cream from the back of a truck and Jerry scooped ice cream in his college cafeteria. Ben and Jerry moved to Burlington, Vermont, in 1977. When they got there, they decided that they wanted to start a business. Since they both knew ice cream, they started an ice cream parlor in an empty gas station.

Ben and Jerry are known for making great ice cream. Some of their ice cream flavors are out of the ordinary: pickle, garlic, and others. Of all the flavors, Chocolate Chip Cookie Dough is the best-seller. Not only do Ben and Jerry make delicious ice

cream, they're also good examples of Jewish Americans who give back to their community. Ben and Jerry donate 7.5 percent of their profits to charities for building parks, playgrounds, bridges, and baseball fields.

SHORT BIOGRAPHIES

Issac Mayer Wise (1819–1900)

Rabbi Issac Mayer Wise was a man who believed in change. He was born in Steinberg, Bohemia, in 1819. Rabbi Wise's father was a teacher who taught his son all he knew about the Jewish religion.

On July 23, 1840, Rabbi Wise moved to America. While in America, he became a leader in the Jewish Reform Movement, which is a way of practicing Judaism in a more modern way. Rabbi Wise believed that good Jews didn't need to keep kosher, wear traditional clothing, or pray in Hebrew. The Jews in America who agree with Rabbi Wise are members of Reform synagogues today.

Rabbi Wise died on March 26, 1900. He was an important leader in the Jewish community and his work will be always be remembered.

Levi Strauss (1829–1902)

Have you ever worn Levi jeans? Have you ever wonder who invented them? It all started in 1829 in Germany when Levi Strauss was born.

Levi Strauss' career started during the California Gold Rush of 1849. Mr. Strauss took a steam cruiser to San Francisco. He sold canvas, a kind of thick cloth. By the time he reached San Francisco, he had sold all but one bundle of canvas. He hoped to sell his last bundle to a tent maker. Just before he had the chance, a gold miner came up to Mr. Strauss, asking him for durable pants because pants tore easily in the mines.

Being a good salesman, Mr. Strauss took the canvas to a tailor to make it into pants. Then he sold them to the miner. The miner bragged to all his friends how his pants were so great. All the miners from his camp wanted to have pants like his. The word soon spread around California. Mr. Strauss realized that he would need a better cloth than canvas. He picked denim. Across the world his pants were becoming famous. This was the beginning

Levi Strauss

of his blue jean business that is still popular today.

Henrietta Szold (1860–1945)

Henrietta Szold was born in Baltimore, Maryland, on December 21, 1860. She came from a large family and was the daughter of a rabbi. Henrietta's father taught her about the Jewish faith. Ms. Szold did many important things. She started *Hadassah*—an organization responsible for creating clinics, hospitals, and medical, dental, and nursing schools in Palestine. She also saved the lives of several thousand Jewish children from the Holocaust through the Youth Aliyah Program. This organization helped children who would have been killed in Nazi concentration camps.

Ms. Szold didn't live to see the birth of the Jewish state of Israel, but her memory lives on through Hadassah, and through the lives of the children she saved in the Youth Aliyah Program. This program still exists today, helping children in areas of the world where it is unsafe because of fighting.

George Burns (1896–1996)

Comedians can be very funny, but most retire long before they are 100 years old! Not George Burns!

Mr. Burns' real name was Nathan Bernbaum. He was born in New York on January 20, 1896. He started doing part-time jobs when he was very young. Sometimes, while selling crackers, he would add some show-biz to his work, such as singing. He developed skills in trick roller

George Burns (left) and Gracie Allen (middle)

skating and acting on the Vaudeville stage. When he was 14, he experienced stage fright and decided he needed a security object. He chose a cigar, which became his trademark.

Mr. Burns spent several more years doing small shows until he met Gracie Allen. Mr. Burns and Ms. Allen did many shows together, and they got married in 1926. George Burns was in a variety of radio and television programs and made several movies.

George Burns passed away shortly after his 100th birthday. We will always remember this man who made us laugh.

Golda Meir (1898–1978)

Golda Meir was the first woman prime minister of Israel. She was born on May 3, 1898, in Russia. Her family was very poor. Her father came home one night and said he was tired of their harsh lifestyle. He decided to move the family to America.

In 1906, Golda Meir's family moved to Milwaukee, Wisconsin. When she got a little older, she got a marriage proposal from a wealthy man. Her parents wanted her to accept the man's proposal and leave school, but her sister advised her not to. Golda listened to her sister. She didn't want to get married yet. She ran away to Denver, completed her education in 1917, and then she got married.

In 1921, Ms. Meir decided to move to Israel and try to become the first woman prime minister of Israel. In 1969, she did! When Israel was being attacked by the surrounding Arab countries, Golda Meir went to America to ask Congress for weapons to help the Jews defend themselves from attacks. On May 11, 1948, Israel was declared an independent country.

Golda Meir died in 1978. She was a great leader and an example of a Jewish American who worked hard for other people.

Jonas Salk (1914–1995)

Jonas Salk was born in New York in 1914. He went to a high school for gifted boys. In 1934, he attended New York University as a graduate chemistry student. He studied bacteria at college until 1947.

That same year he went to Pittsburgh University where he became the Director of the Virus Research Lab until 1963. Dr. Salk once explained that as he works in his lab, he tries to imagine himself as the object he's studying. Imagine thinking of yourself as a virus or a cancer cell or even as the immune system for the whole body! This thinking process helped him design additional experiments.

Dr. Salk supervised experiments that led to the discovery of a vaccine to prevent polio in 1954. Polio is a disease that eats away at a person's muscular system. When the polio vaccine worked, Dr. Salk's name became internationally known. He won four awards for his work on polio, including the Nobel Prize. When he died in 1995, he was searching for a cure for the deadly disease AIDS.

Henry Kissinger (b. 1923)

An American president has many advisors. An advisor is a person who gives the president advice. Henry Kissinger was one of the most influential advisors ever. Dr. Kissinger was born on May 23, 1923, in Germany. In 1938, the Kissinger family left Germany and came to the United States. In 1943, he became an American citizen and was drafted into the army. After he was discharged, he earned his Ph.D. from Harvard University.

In 1969, Dr. Kissinger was chosen as

Henry Kissinger

the assistant to former President Richard Nixon for National Security Affairs. He later became secretary of state. Today, Dr. Kissinger is a director of the International Rescue Committee. He has won several awards, including the Nobel Peace Prize, the Presidential Medal of Freedom, and the Medal of Liberty. Dr. Kissinger is someone who has dedicated his life to serving the United States.

Barbara Walters (b. 1931)

Barbara Walters has been doing "20/20" and the "Barbara Walters' Special" TV programs for many years. She was born on September 25, 1931. After high school she went to college and received a Bachelor of Arts degree in English. When Ms. Walters started working, she wanted to be an actress. After many jobs, she was invited to host "The Today Show." Then she covered several important stories, such as Jacqueline Kennedy's 1962 trip to India. In 1977, she got an interview with the president of Egypt, Anwar Sadat, and Israeli Prime Minister Menachem Begin, after their historic peace treaty.

Barbara Walters is part of a Jewish family. She's most proud of the work she has done covering the Middle East peace process. Of all the people she has met, her heroes are those who work with people with disabilities.

Leonard Nimoy (b. 1931)

Ever heard of *Star Trek*? We're talking about the first *Star Trek* series, with Leonard Nimoy, known on the show as Mr. Spock.

Leonard Nimoy

Leonard Nimoy was born to Russian immigrants in Boston, Massachusetts, on March 26, 1931. He grew up in a kosher home. Today, Mr. Nimoy still visits his parents to celebrate Passover and doesn't work on the High Holy Holidays.

Leonard Nimoy is a famous actor, a drama teacher, and a director. He starred in all the *Star Trek* movies and several other films. He directed *Star Trek III: The Search for Spock* and *Star Trek IV: The Voyage Home.*

Shel Silverstein (b. 1932)

Shel Silverstein has written many wonderful books—something for everyone. One favorite is the remarkable story of a tree that gives all it can to a man. That book is called *The Giving Tree.*

Shel Silverstein was born in Chicago in 1932. He liked to sing and compose songs as he grew up. Mr. Silverstein said he wanted to be a baseball player or be popular with girls. Since he was neither, he started drawing and writing. Mr. Silverstein always illustrates his own books. *The Giving Tree, A Light in the Attic,* and *Where the Sidewalk Ends* are some of the books he has written and illustrated for kids. Shel Silverstein is still writing and making us laugh every time we read his work.

Ruth Bader Ginsburg (b. 1933)

Hear ye! Hear ye! Order in the court. Listen and read about the life of Ruth Bader Ginsburg.

She was born in Brooklyn, New York, in 1933. When Ms. Ginsburg attended Harvard Law School, she was one of only nine women in a class of 500 students. She finished her studies at Columbia Law School. When Ms. Ginsburg graduated from law school, she tied for first place in her class in academic achievement. She was destined for great things. Her goal was to be a judge.

Ms. Ginsburg has always fought against racism and for women's rights. She helped many people as a U.S. Court of Appeals Justice. In 1993, Ms. Ginsburg was nominated to the Supreme Court. As the first Jewish woman in the Supreme Court, Ruth Bader Ginsburg is an inspiration and a positive role model for many young people.

Judy Blume (b. 1938)

Have you ever heard of *Freckle Juice, Tales of a Fourth Grade Nothing,* or *Superfudge?* If you've read one of these stories, then you know about one of the greatest children's authors, Judy Blume.

Ms. Blume isn't sure how she became an author. It just happened. She takes an honest approach to everyday situations in her books. She thinks that young people need to know there are others out in the world with the same kinds of problems they are experiencing. That's why in most of her books she deals with the problems of young people. Judy Blume's books are still popular today because most kids can relate to what she writes about and they really enjoy her humor.

Barbra Streisand

Barbra Streisand (b. 1942)

"People who need people are the luckiest people in the world . . . " sings Barbra Streisand in one of her most famous songs. She is a successful singer, actress, director, and producer.

Barbra Streisand was born on April 24, 1942, in a Jewish section of Brooklyn, New York. She received two Grammy Awards for Best Album and Best Female Vocalist. She went on to win many awards for her work in movies. She still wins awards for her work in show business. She is one of Hollywood's most talented stars.

Barbra Streisand will be remembered for her wonderful singing voice, her producing and directing, and her contributions of time and money to humanitarian causes, saving the environment, and the state of Israel.

Mark Spitz (b. 1950)

Can you imagine what it would be like to win a gold medal in the Olympic Games? Well, Mark Spitz can! He was born in 1950. He learned to swim when he was six. By the time he was eight, he swam 75 minutes a day.

Mark Spitz started swimming more and more. His first award-winning year was in 1967. That year he won five gold medals in the Pan American Games in Winnipeg, Canada. His best year ever was 1972 at the Munich Olympics where he won seven gold medals, setting a new Olympic record in every swimming event he entered.

Swimmer Mark Spitz is known as one of the greatest Jewish athletes of all time. He is now a member of the Jewish Hall of Fame in Israel. "I feel that being a Jewish athlete has helped our cause," he says. "We have shown that we are as good as the next guy."

Jerry Seinfeld (b. 1954)

Jerry Seinfeld was born in New York. After college, he started performing in small comedy clubs and then became a regular on *The Tonight Show*. Today he stars in the popular television show *Seinfeld*.

Jerry Seinfeld is one of America's favorite comedians on television. Mr. Seinfeld is a unique kind of comedian. He wants to keep his head clear, so he never drinks alcohol or smokes cigarettes. According to Mr. Seinfeld, bad language is not needed to make people laugh. Instead, he uses his clever observations about people and everyday life to entertain and amuse his audiences.

Jerry Seinfeld is a good example of how people can lead a healthy lifestyle and still have fun. His Jewish background is important to him, so twice a month he and his close Jewish friends meet in one of their homes with two rabbis to study Talmud. We think it's great that someone well known and popular makes religion a priority in his life.

MORE FAMOUS FIRSTS AND HEROES

Here is a list of a some more famous Jewish Americans. You may not have heard of these people, but you can learn more by visiting your school or local library. We have arranged these people by the year of their birth. These are only some of the many famous Jewish Americans.

Salomon, Haym (1740–1785)
One of the financiers of the American Revolution.

Gratz, Rebecca (1781–1869)
Founder of the Philadelphia Orphan Asylum; founder and director of the first Hebrew Sunday School in America.

Jacobs, Francis W. (1843–1892)
Founder of the National Jewish Hospital and the National United Way.

Bernhardt, Sarah (1844–1923)
Dramatic actress.

Pulitzer, Joseph (1847–1911)
Leading newspaper publisher; endowed money for the Pulitzer Prize.

Gompers, Samuel (1850–1924)
Founder and first president of the American Federation of Labor (AFL).

Berliner, Emile (1851–1929)
German American inventor. Created the gramophone and the microphone. Led national efforts to fight tuberculosis.

Michelson, Albert (1852–1931)
First American scientist to win a Nobel Prize—father of modern theoretical physics.

Brandeis, Louis (1856–1941)
First Jewish Supreme Court Judge, 1916.

Boas, Franz (1858–1942)
Helped develop the study of humankind known as anthropology.

Ochs, Adolph (1858–1935)
One of the original developers of the New York Times.

Rubenstein, Helena (1872–1965)
American businesswoman. Established a new industry—cosmetics.

Stein, Gertrude (1874–1946)
Twentieth-century writer.

Mayer, Louis B. (1885–1957)
Head of Metro-Goldwyn-Mayer (MGM), one of the originators of the American motion picture industry.

Waksman, Dr. Selman (1888–1973)
Discovered antibiotics and won the Nobel Prize.

Marx, Groucho (1890–1977)
Comedian.

Sarnoff, David (1891–1971)
Developed RCA, the Radio Corporation of America, and its subsidiary NBC, the National Broadcasting Corporation.

Gershwin, George (1898–1937)
A giant in classical, popular, and jazz music; wrote over 2,000 songs.

Eisenstaedt, Alfred (1898–1995)
Father of photojournalism. Famous for his *Life* magazine covers.

Playwright Neil Simon

Rickover, Hyman G. (1900–1986)
Father of the atomic-powered submarine.

Rothko, Mark (1903–1970)
Artist. One of the leaders of the school of Abstract Expressionism in New York.

Sabin, Dr. Albert Bruce (b. 1906)
Polish American microbiologist who developed an oral vaccine against polio.

Goodman, Benny (1909–1986)
Known as the "King of Swing." Played clarinet, was a bandleader, overcame racial barriers by asking African Ameri can musicians to play with his band.

Miller, Arthur (b. 1915)
Playwright. Best known for the plays *Death of a Salesman* and *The Crucible*.

Handler, Ruth (b. 1916)
Created the Barbie and Ken dolls.
Started Mattel Toy Company.

Yalow, Dr. Rosalyn (b. 1921)
A former secretary, she won the Nobel
Prize in Medicine in 1977.

Carlebach, Shlomo (1925–1994)
Rabbi and musician. Used music to
reunite many non-practicing Jews with
their religion and culture.

Brooks, Mel (b. 1926)
Director, producer, and actor in television shows and movies.

Simon, Neil (b. 1927)
Well-known playwright for Broadway
and film.

Sondheim, Stephen (b. 1930)
Known for musicals such as *A Funny
Thing Happened on the Way to the
Forum* and *Sweeney Todd.*

Diamond, Neil (b. 1941)
A popular songwriter-singer. Film debut
in *The Jazz Singer*, a remake of the original Al Jolson film.

Dylan, Bob (b. 1941)
Songwriter and singer. Known for his
rock 'n' roll and folk music.

Simon, Paul (b. 1942)
Songwriter and singer.

REAL PEOPLE

Real Jewish people in America today
Tell wonderful stories
In their own special way.
They may do something
Different than you,
But these great people
Are special, too.

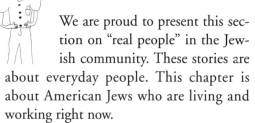

We are proud to present this section on "real people" in the Jewish community. These stories are about everyday people. This chapter is about American Jews who are living and working right now.

After interviewing these men and women, we discovered that they are proud of their heritage and enjoy helping others. They are people who started their own companies, who moved here from other countries, and who live in big cities or small towns. They are people who enjoy their lives and feel very lucky to be American Jews.

We would like to thank everyone for taking time to answer our questions, especially those who came to our workshop to be interviewed. The people we interviewed were interesting, and we hope you enjoy their true life experiences. We think you will give this chapter "two thumbs up!"

LES SHAPIRO

Are you interested in sports? Well, Les Shapiro is. He is a newscaster for Channel 4 in Denver, Colorado. He is exciting to listen to and has a great sense of humor. For example, when we asked him how large his family was, he raised his hands and showed us how tall they were. That wasn't quite the answer we expected! Then he told us that when all his relatives get together, there are about 120 people. His family is so big that he can't even remember all their names.

Les Shapiro

Les Shapiro and his family feel lucky to be citizens of the United States. His mother's family left Germany in 1937 during the rise of Hitler. Mr. Shapiro's father-in-law, Jack Ashley, was from Lodz, Poland. He avoided being used in Nazi medical experiments on children by stuffing his shirt with newspaper to look like an adult. Although Jack Ashley lost many of his family members during this time, he was finally released when the war was over.

From the time Les was nine until he was 13, he went to Hebrew school four days a week until his Bar Mitzvah. His grandfather arranged the music for the Bar Mitzvah party. Was it rock 'n' roll? No! It was accordion music. Les wondered how anyone could dance to that kind of music. He didn't like it.

When Mr. Shapiro was young, he liked going to family picnics, Purim parties, big family events, and playing softball in the streets. He also enjoyed playing with his friends. Some of his friends were Jewish and some were not. His best friend, Scott, happens to be Jewish and they are still great friends today.

On Yom Kippur, Jewish adults often fast for the entire day. Mr. Shapiro didn't grow up in an Orthodox home and chose not to fast. His cousin Gary, who was spending the night, was more observant and was fasting. Les took a chicken leg out of the refrigerator and teased his cousin while chasing him around the house. His cousin got really upset and Les was sent to his room for a few hours. Les never teased Gary like that again!

After Les Shapiro graduated from Arizona State University, he sent out tapes of himself broadcasting. One place in Dallas told him that they loved his broadcast, but that he looked too ethnic. Mr. Shapiro figured it was just a polite way to say that he was too Jewish. He then thought briefly about changing his name, but decided that if the news station didn't accept him because of who he was, he didn't want to work for them. Les Shapiro realized he is proud of his name and proud to be Jewish!

Les Shapiro and his wife, Paula, met in high school. They were good friends for ten years before they started dating. Mr. Shapiro secretly had a crush on Paula for all those years, but he was very patient. They finally started dating and fell in love.

Now they have two boys, Cary and Jessie. Since Mr. Shapiro works at least 60 hours a week, he doesn't have much time to spend with his children. When he has the day off, he likes to spend it with his family. His children are the most important part of his life. He loves to read to them, play ball with them, make them breakfast, and take them to school.

The Shapiros attend a synagogue near their home on the Jewish High Holy days. Their children go to a Jewish study group to learn more about their heritage. Mr. and Mrs. Shapiro try to teach their children to get along. They know that they will appreciate each other when they grow up.

The most important message Les Shapiro had for us is to be who we are because we can't change it! He said you shouldn't let people bother you for being Jewish or a member of any other religion. Respect your family and yourself.

"Don't idolize sports people just because they might do one or two things well. Enjoy watching them during the game, but respect them because they are good at heart!"

THE SOBOL FAMILY

Theresa met Joel Sobol on a boat going to Crete. The year was 1975 and Joel had been traveling around Europe. The next thing they knew, they were back at Theresa's house together—quite a surprise for her German Catholic parents!

Three years later, Theresa and Joel got married in America. Their parents weren't happy about the idea at first, because their children were different religions. But eventually they got used to it. In 1980, Theresa and Joel had a daughter, named Ilana. In 1984, they had a son named Michael. Little Ilana wasn't sure having a brother was much of a blessing. Now she had to share her parents!

We asked them what it was like for one of them to be Jewish and the other Catholic. Did either of them consider changing religions? What about their children? Did they celebrate Hanukkah or Christmas? Did they attend a church or a synagogue?

On the question of conversion, Joel said, "It never entered my mind." He grew up in the United States, went to a Jewish

Ilana and Michael Sobol in Nazareth, Israel.

school, attended synagogue regularly, and had a Bar Mitzvah ceremony. Then he went through a time when he didn't feel as though he belonged anywhere. After traveling through Europe and northern Africa, he went to Israel. He said that the emotional connection there was so strong "it was like coming home."

Theresa was raised in a Catholic home in Germany. Spending time with Joel in Israel has helped her understand Judaism. She feels comfortable with the Jewish religion, but has never considered converting.

Today, the family lives in Golden, Colorado, and is in a program for Jewish interfaith families called Stepping Stones. An interfaith family means that one parent is Jewish and the other one is not. Stepping Stones has helped the Sobols a lot. It is a place where kids can do cooking, art projects, and also make new friends.

They have had to decide on family traditions. At first, Joel was shocked about putting up a Christmas tree. But he realized that it was very important to Theresa. Now they celebrate Catholic *and* Jewish holidays in their home. They say that you have to make compromises when you are part of an interfaith family. Thanks to Stepping Stones, this is something the Sobols have learned to enjoy doing. Ilana and Michael highly recommend the Stepping Stones program to other kids and their parents.

The Sobol kids enjoy having two religious backgrounds because they have the best of both worlds. They have had an opportunity to learn about different reli-

gions and to attend different places of worship. Their parents have taught them values that are common to both religions, including being kind, being honest, and doing the best that you can.

The Sobols are happy with their family life and wouldn't change anything. They believe that open communication is important to help people become more understanding of differences. That's something everyone can work for.

ROSLYN BRESNICK-PERRY

Roslyn Bresnick-Perry was born in Russia on August 8, 1922. She grew up in a mostly Jewish town. Roslyn said that she had two different childhoods. One was in Russia, where she lived only with her

Roslyn Bresnick-Perry

mother. Her father left Russia when Roslyn was only six months old to go to America to find a better life for his family. When her father finally became an American citizen, he was able to bring his wife and Roslyn to America. By that time, Roslyn had already turned seven.

Roslyn always wanted to be a real American girl, but it was not easy. When Roslyn came to America, it was the time of the Great Depression which meant that many people were very poor. Rosalyn's family didn't have much money or food. She missed her grandparents, aunts, uncles, and cousins in Russia. She says that her brother and sister, who were born in America, helped her have fun.

Two things that Roslyn missed most when she came to America were trees and flowers. In Russia there were lots of trees and flowers. On her street in the Bronx, there weren't any. Roslyn thought that America had no trees, until her friend Angelina told Roslyn about the garden in her backyard. Roslyn really wanted to see the garden, but Angelina didn't think she should show it to her because her grandmother, who only spoke Italian, didn't like people coming to the house.

Roslyn finally convinced Angelina to let her see the garden. The girls were so interested in the garden that they didn't notice that Angelina's grandmother had come outside. She yelled to Angelina in Italian, pointing her finger at Roslyn and calling her a nasty name. Roslyn had to leave right away. Anglina was forbidden to talk to her anymore because Roslyn was Jewish. Roslyn was scared. She didn't understand why someone could hate her because of her heritage. Later, she talked to her father about it and he made her feel better. In the end, Roslyn felt sorry for Angelina's grandmother because she treated people like that.

Ms. Bresnick-Perry has had a very interesting life. Now she is a famous storyteller who tells stories about her Jewish life. In fact, most of her stories come from her childhood. She also likes to tell stories about what being Jewish in America means. Ms. Bresnick-Perry is proud to be a Jewish American. She says that being Jewish is really a "peoplehood" because it is not only a religion, but also a civilization, tradition, and culture.

One of Ms. Bresnick-Perry's heroes growing up was Ethel Holstein, her third grade teacher. She helped Roslyn believe in herself. When Roslyn came to America, she only spoke Yiddish. She had a very hard time learning to read and spell in English because she was dyslexic, which made reading and writing difficult for her. Her teacher worked hard to help her.

Roslyn's family felt it was important to keep their Jewish traditions. But it was also important to be American and speak English. She remembers that education has always been a part of her life. She feels that Jews are "people of the book," and that's why she loves stories so much.

Today, Ms. Bresnick-Perry is married and lives in New York City. She has three sons, two of whom teach college-level drama and music. Ms. Bresnick-Perry feels that she passed on her love of the arts to her children.

Ms. Bresnick-Perry wants to keep Jewish history alive by telling stories. She says that the youth today need to know where their people come from. She also wants them to know that Jewish people are an important part of American history. She hopes that future generations will feel proud of their heritage, too.

ABE AND FRANCES HONIGMAN

Frances and Abe Honigman grew up in Poland. Abe was born in Kelz in 1917 and moved to the city of Lodz when he was four. Frances was born in Lodz in 1920. Fortunately, both of them survived the Holocaust and they were able to immigrate to America. We learned a lot by listening to their story, and we wanted to share it with you.

Frances' family was very Orthodox and very disciplined. Her grandfather was a rabbi. When asked what it was like at her house Frances said, "When my father picked up a spoon, we all did. He was the king." She also lived with her mother, older sister, and two older brothers.

Abe did not consider his family to be as Orthodox or as strict as Frances'. He lived with his mother, father, grandfather, two brothers, and sister. Family was very important to him. He enjoyed playing with his cousins and seeing his aunts and uncles. Sometimes 30 relatives would be at his house together. Abe went to Hebrew school after regular school. That was a lot of school, but he liked learning Hebrew.

Abe and Frances met at a dance when they were teenagers. After the dance, Abe kissed Frances without asking her. Frances smacked him! After that, they continued to see each other and went to dances and movies together.

In early 1939, Frances was in Warsaw with her nephew when the Nazis invaded Poland. She quickly took him to the small town of Kelz to hide from the Nazis. By September, all of the Jews were forced to wear a yellow arm band or patch to indicate that they were Jewish. Her sister and brother-in-law came to Kelz two months later. Frances saw her parents for the last time in December of that year. They died soon after the Nazi invasion.

In 1941, Frances and Abe were engaged. Abe's family also went back to Kelz. Frances and Abe both were forced to work for the Nazis. Abe worked in a stone quarry and Frances worked on a farm. Then the Nazis built a ghetto in Kelz and the family was forced to stay there. Later, many Jews were sent to concentration camps. Many of their relatives were taken away to a concentration camp.

Frances' job was to sort through the clothing left by the Jews who had already been taken away. She sneaked some of the clothes into the ghetto so that they could be sold to buy bread. Jews were not allowed to celebrate any Jewish holidays and were treated very badly. Later, they worked seven days a week in a factory. It is a good thing that Frances was young and healthy. Those who weren't strong enough to work were killed. Every day, Frances had to witness people being executed by the Nazis.

In April of 1944, after three years of ghetto life, Abe and Frances were both sent to a concentration camp called Auschwitz. They were both in the same camp, but didn't know what was happening to the other one.

Finally, on April 25, 1945, the International Red Cross came to free the women at Auschwitz. However, the scared women had been lied to so many times that they didn't want to go with the Red Cross. They didn't trust anyone. The men from the Red Cross finally had to pick the women up, put them in the trucks, and take them to freedom.

Abe was freed May 7, 1945. Two days later he was placed in a hospital. After two weeks, he was released from the hospital and taken to Lund, Sweden. Frances had already been taken to Malmo, Sweden. They were only 30 minutes apart but didn't know that the other was alive. Someone told Frances that Abe might be in Lund. She took a bus and found him.

The Honigmans married and made their home in Sweden for eight years. They lived in a community with other Jews who had lost their homes and left the country where they had lived. Their first two children were born while they lived in Sweden. They came to America on January 14, 1952. Shortly after coming to America, they moved from New York to Youngstown, Ohio. In that town, many Jewish people from Poland met to play cards and have picnics at the lake on Sundays. They began to make new friends, and their youngest son was born in America. That was the beginning of their new American life.

They became American citizens as soon as they could.

They never took English classes, but learned the language very quickly. In 1957, they were able to buy a grocery store. It started out small, but they worked seven days a week and built a good business until they sold the store in 1982. Frances said that after 25 years, she was tired of working so hard in the store.

Abe and Frances have a message to share with people of all ages. Love the children and be willing to sacrifice for them. Also, teach children to believe in education and to build a good future for themselves and their families.

After 50 years of marriage, the Honigmans shared this advice: forgive each other, fight to keep and take care of your loved ones, and don't make decisions when you're angry! They are thankful for their children and grandchildren and for the opportunity to raise them in America without fear.

DORIS KWARTIN

On October 31, 1939, Doris Kwartin was born in New York. Doris is a second generation American Jew. She has two older sisters, Ida and Helen. Her grandparents were from Poland and Russia. She considers herself a Conservative Jewish American. Now she lives in New Jersey.

Doris grew up in an Orthodox Jewish home. She observed both American and Jewish holidays. She lived in a mixed neighborhood and had friends of different religions. Everyone got along just fine.

Doris Kwartin (left) with her son, Mathew, at his wedding

Like other young girls her age, Doris was not given the opportunity to learn Hebrew or attend religious education classes. In that time, it was not considered as important for girls to learn the Torah. As she got older, she started thinking more and more about Judaism. She had a lot of questions and wanted an opportunity to find the answers. At the age of 40, Ms. Kwartin finally learned Hebrew.

When she was young, her hero was her grandfather. He was always loving, caring, and kind. Her grandfather escaped from the religious persecution in Russia around 1905. He stowed away on a ship, jumped overboard, and swam to England. He was very brave. Ms. Kwartin's grandfather was a tailor and he saved his money until he had enough to send for his wife and children, who were still in Russia. Ms. Kwartin's grandfather took time to listen and talk to her. He was very religious. Doris was only 12 when he died.

Growing up, Doris had one goal and that was to be a good Jewish wife and mother. After five weeks of dating, she married a Jewish man named Abraham, now a retired bus driver. Together they had three boys, named Mathew, Louis, and Steven. Doris Kwartin is very close to her family. She believes she has done a good job bringing up her children by passing on the strong beliefs and the heritage of the Jewish culture and faith.

All three of her sons are active in their faith. Mathew and Steve both direct youth programs for their synagogues. Louis is active in his synagogue, too. Only Mathew is married.

We were lucky to get the chance to interview her son Mathew. Mathew told us about how he met and fell in love with Laura, a Catholic girl. Since Mathew is Jewish, when he decided to marry Laura, his family had many concerns and gave him lots of advice. "If a fish and a bird were to fall in love," they said, "where would they make a house?" His parents weren't sure if they wanted their son to marry outside of their religion because of the many differences. Mathew and Laura were married, and now his parents are both very supportive and hope for the best.

Doris Kwartin made her dream of being a wife and mother come true. She and her husband have passed the teaching of the Torah and the Jewish heritage on to their sons. Doris Kwartin continues to strive to be a positive role model for Jewish youth.

RABBI EVE BEN-ORA

Rabbi Eve Ben-Ora lives in Sugar Land, Texas. Her birthday is April 17, 1957. She is a bright Jewish American woman. Rabbi Ben-Ora grew up with her parents and her brother, Daniel, and sister, Miriam, in a non-Jewish neighborhood. She attended public schools, but she also went to Hebrew school three to four times a week in the afternoon. When she was in high school, she joined a Jewish youth group called United Synagogue Youth (USY).

Rabbi Ben-Ora has many special people in her life. When she was younger, she felt her rabbi was a wonderful teacher and that he gave great sermons. When she was 11, she saw a woman read from the Torah and hoped someday she would be able to do that. Rabbi Ben-Ora's mother taught her many important things, such as, "Always leave a place better than how you found it" and "If you kids can't get along, how do you expect there to be peace in the world!" These ideas have helped her as she grew up.

After receiving her college degrees, she spent an additional five years in school to become a rabbi. Rabbi Ben-Ora was the first female rabbi in Colorado. She is happy that people don't seem to care about her gender and have accepted women rabbis. She has chosen to devote her life to teaching Judaism so that others might appreciate its richness and beauty. Her goal is to make Judaism last forever.

Rabbi Ben-Ora feels that being Jewish is a way of feeling more connected to other people who share your history and heritage. She celebrates all the Jewish holidays and has a house full of menorahs and Seder plates. Her family doesn't wear special clothing to celebrate the holidays, but they do wear the traditional tallit (prayer shawl) and kippah (skullcap). On the pulpit, Rabbi Eve Ben-Ora wears a tallit and kippah with a black or white robe depending on the service.

Today, the most important thing in her life is her family. She has been married for 14 years to Avi Schulman. He is also a rabbi. They have three children: Naomi Chana, Carmiel Zvi, and Rebecca Hadar. The children's last names are Ben-Ora

Marcia Ben-Ora

Rabbi Eve Ben-Ora and family

Schulman. Rabbi Ben-Ora wanted the children to have both last names so they would know that they came from both the parents. The naming services of her children were the most meaningful experiences she has had as a Jewish person, because learning about Judaism is the greatest gift you can pass on. She can give this gift to her children like it was given to her by her parents and grandparents. It is something that she deeply cherishes.

Being Jewish has given Rabbi Ben-Ora's life a focus that combines study, prayer, and celebration. It teaches her to look for the best in people and to try to make herself a better person. What is important to Rabbi Ben-Ora is making sure Judaism will continue in both the young and the old. It connects you to many others around the world through celebration and prayer. She feels that future generations should not be deprived of this wonderful gift.

Rabbi Ben-Ora hopes that through Judaism things will change. It is important to keep Judaism alive because it makes the world a better place. She hopes that people will learn about peace. One of Rabbi Ben-Ora's favorite sayings teaches, "Not by might, not by power, but by spirit of cooperation shall we all live in peace."

JAY AND RUDY BOSCOE

During the writing workshop, we met Rudy Boscoe and his son Jay. They told us some entertaining stories about immigration, learning their trade, and running

The Boscoe's bakery. Rudy Boscoe is on the right.

their bagel business. We enjoyed learning about this family and how they have made bagels for years.

The Boscoe family came from Russia in 1895. Rudy's father, Jacob, left Russia because it was not a democracy and he had very few freedoms. He wanted to go where he could be free and his family would be safe. Many other families also left to look for a better life. They came to America because it was known as the "Golden Land" where everyone had rights. Jacob Boscoe was so happy to have found a place where his family was safe that he didn't mind paying taxes. He loved voting and having all kinds of privileges. This is something that Rudy Boscoe remembers even though his father died when he was still very young.

Today, Rudy and Jay Boscoe still feel that it is a privilege to be an American, and they have passed this value on to their children and grandchildren.

In 1906, Rudy's parents bought a bakery in Denver, Colorado. Rudy was born right there in the bakery on February 12, 1908. We think this gave him a great start for being a baker. He feels honored to share a birthday with another great American, Abraham Lincoln.

Rudy grew up in the bakery business. When he was a young boy, he had to stand on a stool in order to take the bread out of the brick oven. At the age of 12, Rudy started making deliveries in a Model A truck. With today's heavy traffic, you wouldn't want a 12-year-old driving a delivery truck would you?

When Rudy became an adult, he married Anne. Rudy and Anne had five children together and they taught them about their Jewish heritage. Like the Boscoe family, Anne's family also emigrated from Russia. Anne's father escaped Russia on foot and walked all the way across Europe. He stopped along the way to work as a horse trainer to make money. In each country he learned the language and tried to blend into the community so that he wouldn't be sent back to Russia. All together, he learned five languages! It took him five years, but he finally caught a ship and sailed to America.

Jay, "The Bagel Man," was born to Rudy and Anne on December 10, 1941. Jay became a baker because he liked the family business. He has been making bagels with his father since he was 15. He learned a lot about baking from his father, and he also went to special schools in Kansas and Chicago to learn more. He was the only one in the family who was interested in being a baker and continuing the family business.

In 1971, Jay and his father started a new bakery, The New York Bagel Boys. People ask them if the bagels are "New York" style. Rudy and Jay say they are even better. They make their bagels like the Eastern European people did even before they immigrated to New York. Jay makes his bagels with malt instead of sugar. This lets diabetics enjoy bagels with the rest of the world.

Because the Boscoes are Jewish they have always kept kosher bakeries. The Boscoes still carry on the Jewish tradition of "taking the Challah." They take a chunk of dough from each batch and save it. At the end of the day, this dough is blessed and burnt to remind them of the time of

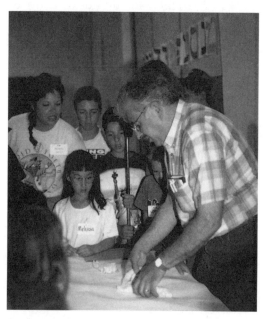

Jay Boscoe

the Temple when Jews gave part of their food as a sacrifice to G-d. Jay's bakery is closed on Jewish holidays and also on American holidays. This gives all his workers time with their families.

Over the years, the Boscoes have observed many changes in the business world. So many people are studying to be doctors and lawyers that Rudy and Jay worry about the trade business going downhill. These professions are very important, but the community also needs qualified people to learn important trades like baking.

Jay and his father, Rudy, have a very unique relationship. Two people who can work together for so many years must be special! Jay and his family hope to continue making bagels for everyone in America to enjoy.

ALYSA STANTON

In the movie *The Lion King*, Mufasa talks to Simba about remembering who you are and the power you have inside you. After meeting Alysa Stanton and hearing about her life, we could tell that this is something she lives by. Her family always told her that she could do anything she wanted to, just as long as she tried. Her message to Jewish youth is to remember who you are.

Alysa Stanton was born August 2, 1963. She is a Jewish African American who has already done a lot in her life. Ms. Stanton did not grow up Jewish, but she became interested in learning about the Jewish religion and, after a lot of searching,

Alysa Stanton

she converted to Judaism at the age of 24. At first her family didn't take her decision to become Jewish seriously, but after she converted they respected her choice. She is actively involved in her temple as an usher and as a teacher to kindergarten and first grade students. She likes to play her guitar and sing songs with children.

Ms. Stanton lived in Ohio until she was 11. She was the youngest of four children and experienced living in a poor area of Cleveland. Later, she moved to Cleveland Heights and went to a neighborhood school where she got all of the Jewish and Christian holidays off. That was the good part. The bad part was that she had to go to school until 4:30 in the afternoon!

When Alysa was a young girl, she wanted to be a doctor, but she didn't think she was smart enough. At age 14 she decided she wanted to be a psychologist. Today she is a psychotherapist. In her job she works with children and families to help heal hearts and spirits. She is also studying to be a nurse practitioner at the University of Colorado. With this degree she will help a regular doctor and be able to do physicals, but not surgery. She hopes to work with the Red Cross, helping people in disasters around the world. Soon she will be Dr. Stanton. Now she knows she is smart enough.

Today Ms. Stanton lives in Denver with her dog named Charles. She celebrates all Jewish holidays and celebrates Christmas with her family. Someday she would also like to start celebrating the African American holiday of Kwanzaa. Ms. Stanton says that being Jewish is hard at times because it's not just a religion, it's a culture and a way of life. She often wears a Star of David necklace, which is a symbol of her religion. Ms. Stanton is proud to be Jewish. She has been waiting for a long time to take a trip to Israel. She hopes to go soon.

If Alysa Stanton could have a wish for the world, it would be that everyone would have food, medical help, and a place to live. She has experienced prejudice in her life as an African American Jew. These experiences have taught her to be respectful of others and to hope that someday everyone will be respectful of other people no matter what their religion or their color of skin might be.

STORIES

Stories are something you can hear,
They make past generations seem near.
"Think before you speak," some stories say.
Valuable lessons that will pay.
When the Jews had nothing left,
Their priceless stories were all they kept.

Stories are an important part of Jewish culture. Even when it was forbidden to practice Judaism, Jewish stories kept going. Even when the Temples were burned and Torahs were taken away, the stories remained because they came from the heart. These stories connected the Jews from one generation to the next.

Stories help teach values to people. Although stories differ from one culture to the next, they often share similar lessons. While reading the stories we've included here, we learned to think before you speak, that everyone has something worthwhile to offer, and that good things come to people who do good things.

Most Jewish stories are folktales, passed on from one generation to another through storytellers. Some stories come from the Talmud and the Midrash. We had the good fortune of meeting a professional storyteller, Cherie Karo Schwartz.

Ms. Schwartz says that she has an angel that sits on one shoulder and her grandmother's spirit sits on the other. They whisper stories to her. "In America and in modern times, people almost forgot about stories because the world got so fast-paced. But in the last few years, people have begun to appreciate stories again because they go from heart to heart and soul to soul," Ms. Schwartz said. She told us that "stories are the mirror and the memory of where we are from, who we are, and what we know."

Listening to stories can be better than watching TV. If you ever get a chance to hear a storyteller, do it! We guarantee you will enjoy it.

THE ALEF-BET

Alef-bet (ah-LEF-bet) is Hebrew for "alphabet." Many stories tell people how important it is for their prayers to come from their hearts. This is a very old story, so it is hard to know exactly where it came from. It has been told many different ways, but it always teaches us that the words a person uses are not as important as being sure your words come from a real love of G-d. The version of the story is from the *Baal Sham Tov*, the Master of the Good Name, from eighteenth-century Europe.

Once upon a time in a village long ago, there lived a poor man. He worked outside all day. One day he got so hungry that he went to his sukkah to get something to eat. It was the holiday of Sukkot. He wanted to say the prayers for that holiday, but he forgot them. Instead he said the Hebrew alef-bet, which was all he could remember.

"G-d," he said, "put these letters together in a prayer that will please you."

The next day he went to the synagogue. He wanted to say prayers for Sukkot, but he couldn't remember them, so again he said the alef-bet out loud to G-d. He asked

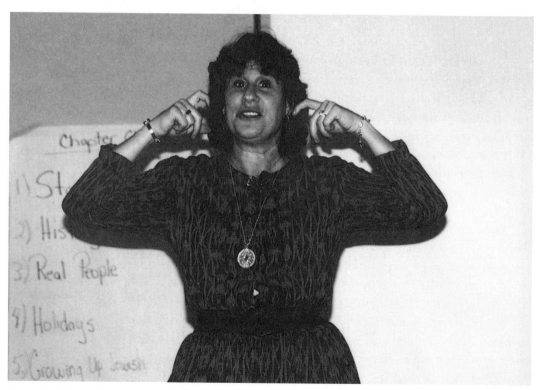

Storyteller Cherie Schwartz

G-d to put them together in a prayer that would be pleasing to Him.

All the people around him got upset. "No, No, No!" they said. "You need to say the correct prayers."

"Stop, stop," said the rabbi. "His prayers are even better than my prayers because he said them from his heart."

This story teaches us that prayers come in all different forms and as long as they come from our heart, G-d will hear them. You might want to see how many different versions of this story you can find in Jewish literature.

THE BOY AND HIS FLUTE

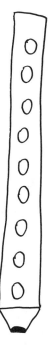

Here is a more recent version of the alef-bet story. It is an Eastern European folktale and has been told in the United States. It also helps us understand that our prayers must come from our hearts.

Once upon a time there lived a boy named Daniel. He was a good boy and worked hard helping his mother take care of his brothers and sisters. His family was poor and lived far away from the synagogue, so he couldn't go there very often. Even though he wanted to, he never learned his Hebrew prayers or the Hebrew language.

One day Daniel heard someone playing a flute. He loved the music so much he decided to make himself a flute so he could play. It took him a long time to make it because he wanted it to be perfect. When he was finally finished, it sounded beautiful. He taught himself to play beautiful songs he made up in his head.

One day he went to school with his brothers and sisters. He wanted to see what he had been missing. When they got to school, all the children were praying in Hebrew. Daniel wanted to offer some kind of prayer to G-d, so he took his flute out of his backpack and began playing a song.

All the children at school were shocked to hear Daniel play his flute while they were praying, but the rabbi smiled and seemed to enjoy listening to Daniel's pleasant music.

The children in the class were upset. "How can you let this happen?" they asked the rabbi. "It is disrespectful to play music while people are praying."

The rabbi said, "Listen up. Daniel's prayers are better than ours because we are just saying the words. His prayer of music is coming from his heart."

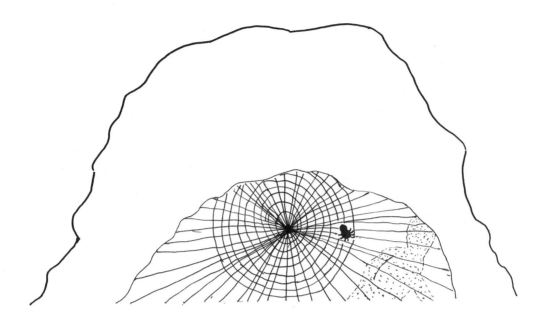

DAVID AND THE SPIDER

Jewish parents tell this story to show how we must respect all G-d's creations. This story is about one of G-d's smallest creatures and how it can be helpful. It is from the *Alphabet of ben Sira.*

Once there lived a shepherd boy. His name was David. He sat and watched a spider spin a web. "What good is a spider?" he asked G-d.

"David," answered G-d, "the time will come when you will need this creature." David was friends with King Saul's son Jonathan, and when he grew up he married Saul's daughter Michal. King Saul was jealous of David, so he ordered his soldiers to capture him. Michal woke David and told him she felt that something bad was going to happen. She told David to run far away until the danger passed.

David ran until he found a cave. He went into a corner of the cave to hide. He sat against the rock wall with his legs close to his chest. "I am doomed!" he said.

"I'll help you," said a little spider.

"How can you help me?" said David. "You're so little!"

The spider started spinning a web over the doorway. The spider worked very hard making the web as fast as it could.

Later, King Saul came to the cave and looked at the huge spider's web. "No one is in here or else this huge spider web would be broken."

Saul and his men continued looking for David, but they never found him. David thanked G-d for creating the spider who could make beautiful webs.

Just to answer your curiosity, David eventually became the king of Israel and did a great job. He wrote the Psalms and killed a giant named Goliath. But those are other stories.

ELIJAH AND THE POOR MAN'S WISH

Elijah was a Jewish prophet. He helped people in need and all those who lived a good life. He is still widely known and respected among Jewish people. There are many folktales about Elijah. Here is one that was found in the Israel Folktale Archives, recorded from Izmir.

Once upon a time there lived a blind old man. He lived with his wife, who saw the world for him. They were very poor and didn't have any children. Most of the time they were very lonely.

One day the old man decided to sit in a green meadow beside a clear, clean river. All of a sudden, he heard the tapping of a cane, and the rustling of a coat, and there was a smell like every smell in the Garden of Eden.

"Do you know who I am?" asked the man who sat down next to him.

"Are you Elijah?" asked the old man.

"Yes," answered Elijah. "I'm here because you have lived a good life even though you are old, blind, poor, and have no children. I will grant you one wish."

The old man's head was spinning so fast he didn't know what to wish for.

"Come back tomorrow at the same place and time," said Elijah, "and I will grant your wish."

So the old man went home and told his wife everything that had happened.

"Here, have dinner," said the man's wife. "Then go to bed and have sweet dreams. Tomorrow I will tell you what to wish for." The kind old woman had guided her husband well for all of the years of their marriage, so he trusted her to come up with a wise wish.

The next day the old man went back to the beautiful river. Again he heard the tapping of the cane, and the rustling of the coat, and smelled every smell in the Garden of Eden. "Yesterday I asked you a question," Elijah said. "Today I would like an answer."

The old man answered him, "I wish to live to see the day my child eats from a golden plate."

"That is a very wise wish!" said Elijah. "I assure you that every part of your wish will be granted."

Remember, it's important to think before you wish. The old man got four things out of one wish because he wished carefully. Can you figure out what they are? Hint: One of the wishes is long life.

WHY IT IS IMPORTANT TO PLANT CAROB TREES

Honi was a miracle worker. He would draw a circle on the ground and then sit in it and pray. He could make miracles happen this way. One day Honi was walking through the forest near a village and he saw an old man planting a tree. "What kind of tree are you planting?" asked Honi. The man told him it was a carob tree. Carob is sort of like a chocolate fruit.

"How long does a carob tree take to grow fruit?" asked Honi.

"It takes 70 years."

"Who is this tree going to be here for? You will be long dead."

"Then my great-grandchildren will enjoy its fruit, as I've enjoyed the fruit of this tree which was planted long ago."

Honi still wondered why the old man would plant a carob tree, because the old man would die long before it grew fruit.

Honi picked a piece of fruit off a grown carob tree. But when he bit into it, he fell into an enchanted sleep that lasted for 70 years.

When he awoke, he saw that everything was different. The tree that the old man had planted was full grown. He saw a child picking off pieces of fruit from the carob tree and eating them.

"Where is the old man who planted that tree yesterday?" Honi asked the child.

"You must be mistaken. My great-grandfather planted this tree 70 years ago."

As Honi watched the child enjoy the carob fruit, he finally understood why the old man had planted that tree.

This story teaches us that it's important to plan for the future. It is from the Talmud, Ta'arit 23a.

THE DONKEY, A CANDLE, AND A ROOSTER

There are many stories in Jewish folklore that teach us that G-d makes things happen for the best. Whether it is today in

America or long ago, we can still learn from the things that happen to us. If we really look carefully, we will find everything is for the best.

Many stories are told about Rabbi Akiva, who believes G-d knows best. Rabbi Akiva traveled all around the country. Sometimes he would collect money for the poor. Sometimes he tried to convince the Roman rulers to change unfair laws. This story is from the Talmud, Berachot 60b.

Once, Rabbi Akiva took a donkey with him on his journey. He had loaded the donkey with everything he would need to survive: a blanket, food, water, and a candle so he could read the Torah at night. He also took a rooster with him because he felt best if he studied early in the morning and the rooster could wake him up.

One day the rabbi was leading his donkey down a long mountain road. Soon it became dark. Luckily, there was a town nearby. So he went into the town to find a place to sleep. When he reached an inn, he asked if they had a room. "No," they said. So he continued on his way.

As it got darker, Rabbi Akiva reached a mansion. He asked for a room there. They told him that they never took in people they didn't know. He set off to find another place, but every place he went to turned him away.

He was standing there looking very sad, with his rooster and donkey, and he started to talk to himself. "Everything G-d does," he said, "He does for the best."

Then he looked around and he saw an open field. He decided to make his camp there. He lit his candle, opened his Torah, fed his rooster and his donkey, and prepared himself to study the Torah. While he was studying, along came a strong wind and blew out his candle. "Everything G-d does," he said to himself again, "He does for the best."

When the rabbi was almost asleep, he was disturbed by a bunch of loud animal sounds. He woke up quickly to see a

mountain lion carrying the donkey away. It made the rabbi very sad, but once again he said, "Everything G-d does, He does for the best."

As he was about to go to sleep again, he awoke once more to hear the squawking from his rooster. It was not a mountain lion this time, but a sly weasel who had stolen his rooster. Never before had the rabbi had such bad luck on a journey. "But everything G-d does," he repeated, "He does for the best."

He went to sleep and the rest of the night was quiet. He woke up in the morning, opened his Torah and said a morning prayer, and began to study. Later, Rabbi Akiva went into town. He knew something was wrong right away because windows were shattered, and wood and doors were lying in the street. He didn't see any men on their way to work. He didn't hear the sounds of children playing in the streets.

Just then the rabbi saw another hiker. He asked if he knew what had happened. The hiker said that thieves had come and kidnapped the villagers and stolen their farm animals and all their belongings.

Then the rabbi realized why he had such bad luck the night before. If the donkey hadn't been eaten by the mountain lion, and if his rooster hadn't been taken by the weasel, they would have made noise and let the robbers know where he was. If somebody would have given him a place to stay, the robbers would surely have taken him captive, too.

The rabbi then said to himself for the last time "Everything G-d does, He does for the best." He gave thanks to G-d for letting him continue on his journey.

Rabbi Akiva teaches us that we should make the best of bad situations because we can learn a lesson from everything G-d does for us.

THE THREE LOAVES

There once was a little old wrinkled lady who lived by the sea. She was very poor, but she was always willing to help others. One day she had just baked three buttery loaves of bread when someone knocked on the door. She got up and opened it. There, standing in front of her, was a very old and frail hungry beggar.

"Please, may I have some food?" he asked the woman.

"Yes!" said the old woman. And off she went to get a loaf of bread for the man.

When the beggar had gotten his bread, he said thank you and went on his way. Just when she was about to sit down, there was another knock at the door. She went to open it and there was another beggar. His clothes were ripped and his face was dirty with mud. He also asked for a loaf of bread. The woman gladly gave the man her second loaf of bread.

She had just sat down again and was about to slice her last loaf of bread when she heard a third knock. She opened the door. It was another beggar asking for food. She was very nice and gave up her last piece of food.

The old woman went out to get some wheat to make some more bread. As she came back to her house, a gust of wind blew her bag of wheat out to the sea. At the same time, there was a ship sailing in the sea. When lightning struck a hole in their ship, the sailors tried filling the hole, but they couldn't plug it. Just then, the old woman's bag of wheat flew into the hole.

"Why, that bag came at just the right time!" said the sailors.

When the old woman's bag flew out of her hands, she was disappointed and mad, so she decided to go see King Solomon, who was known as the wisest king. After all, she had been told that good things happen to those who do good.

It was a long walk to Solomon's palace, but worth it. When she got to the palace, she saw ten sailors all dripping wet. They told the king the story about the wheat sack and the storm. The king kindly asked the sailors to hold up the sack. They held up the sack and the old women recog-nized it as her own. She was given a sack of gold as a reward for helping others!

This story is from *Ma'asim Tovim* ("Good Stories").

THE CLEVER CHILD

Once upon a time, there lived an old man and his three sons. One day the old man called his sons to come to his house. He told his three sons that he couldn't take care of the farm and house anymore because he would soon die. "Each of you take one gold coin," he told his sons. "Go to the market and buy something you think would fill up a whole room." He told them that the son who was able to fill up the whole room with whatever he could buy with just the one coin would get all of his money.

The oldest son ran out and bought some hay for the horses. The second son thought for a while, then he also ran out the door. He went to the market and bought as many flowers as he could hold. The youngest son thought and thought and thought for a long time. Then, at last, he went to a gift shop and bought two lit-tle boxes.

They all came back that night and sat in front of their father. He told them to show what they bought. The oldest son spread out hay for the horses and it filled one corner. The second son spread out his flowers. They smelled good and looked pretty, but the flowers only filled up half of the room.

The youngest son put one box in the middle of the floor and pulled out another box. He took a candle out of the first box and lit it with a match from the second box. The candle filled up the whole room with bright light. The father said to his youngest son, "You are my cleverest child! You will get everything of mine!"

Even though the youngest son was cleverer than his brothers, he shared all of the things with them because he loved them. This story teaches us to think carefully before we act. It is an Ethiopian folktale, which is also told by non-Jews in Ethiopia.

We hope you have enjoyed these stories we have retold in our own words. There are many other stories you may enjoy reading about and sharing. Here is a list of some of

the books we took these stories from. Check one of these out from your local library and enjoy some more stories with your family and friends.

BIBLIOGRAPHY

Here are a few collections of Jewish stories that you might find interesting:

Certner, Simon. *101 Jewish Stories.* (New York: BJE of Greater New York, 1987)

Frankel, Ellen. *The Classic Tales: 4,000 Years of Jewish Lore.* (Jason Aronson, Inc., 1989)

Goldin, Barbara Diamond. *A Child's Book of Midrash.* (Jason Aronson, Inc., 1990)

Schram, Peninnah. *Jewish Stories One Generation Tells Another.* (Jason Aronson, Inc., 1989)

Here is a list of five of our favorite children's books to share with your classmates and family:

Aronin, Ben. *The Secret of the Sabbath Fish.* (Philadelphia: Jewish Publication Society of America, 1978)

Adler, David. *The House on the Roof.* (New York: Bonim Books, 1976)

Heller, Linda. *The Castle on Hester Street.* (Philadelphia: Jewish Publication Society of America, 1982)

Levitin, Sonia. *A Sound to Remember.* (New York: Harcourt Brace Jovanich, 1979)

Schwartz, Cherie Karo. *My Lucky Dreidel.* (New York: Smithmark Publishers, 1994)

LANGUAGE

Part of the fun of learning about another culture is learning about its language. The Jewish culture has Hebrew as its oldest language. There are 23 letters and Hebrew is written from right to left. Today, this formal Hebrew language is usually used to study the Bible and other religious books, and for praying.

The spoken language of the Jewish people has a history all its own. The most common spoken language the Jewish people used is known as Yiddish. This language developed from mixing Hebrew and German. Some French, Polish, and Russian words were also mixed into Yiddish, but the strongest influence is from German. This is because so many Jews settled around Germany when they left their homeland. Other Jewish communities around the world developed their own language.

In our summer workshop, we learned what the Hebrew letters look and sound like. We also learned a few Hebrew and Yiddish words. It was fun to discover that many of these words we already knew. We had heard our parents or grandparents use some of them. Sometimes people use the words to spice up their conversation! We think you will recognize a lot of these words or phrases, too.

Yiddish and Hebrew	English
Bubeleh (BUB-eh-leh) "How are you feeling, bubeleh?"	Little one
Bubbeh (BU-beh) The children's Bubbeh will come to visit soon.	Grandmother
Challah (HAH-lah) We will have a challah for our Shabbat dinner.	Braided bread
Chutzpah (HOOTZ-pah) It took a lot of chutzpah to get up in front of the class and speak.	Nerve or guts
Kosher (KO-sher) Something about this situation is not quite kosher.	Proper
L'Chayim (leh-HI-yim) "*L'chayim!*" they said, raising their glasses to toast the wedding couple.	"To life!"
Mazel Tov (MAH-zul TOV) "*Mazel tov* to you and your family."	"Congratulations!" or "Good luck!"
Mensch (mensh) My teacher is a real mensch.	A good-hearted, decent person

Mishmash (MISH-mash)
We mixed several ingredients together to
make this mishmash.

Concoction

Mitzvah (MITS-vah)
It is a mitzvah to visit sick people.

Commandment or good deed

Nosh (nahsh)
My mom doesn't let us nosh between meals.

Snack

Nudge (nuhj)
My brother keeps nudging me.

Pester

Oy vey!
Oy vey! The box of candy just fell onto the
kitchen floor!

Exclamation similar to "Oh, no!"

Schmaltzy (SHMALT-see)
The story about the boy and his sick dog
was pretty schmaltzy.

Too sentimental

Shalom (shah-LOHM)
Shalom to all my friends.

Hello, goodbye, peace

Shul (shool)
We go to shul every week.

Synagogue

Spiel (shpeel)
What's his spiel?

Story

Tush (toosh)
"Get your tush inside this house right now!"

Rear end

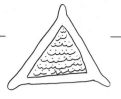

HANDS-ON FUN

Crafts, games, and food you'll meet.
For each celebration there is a treat.
On Passover there's charoset, on Shabbat gefilte fish,
Traditional foods are part of each dish.

In this chapter we teach you how to make some crafts, play some games, and prepare some Jewish foods. We also say what "keeping kosher" means. In this activities chapter, there are instructions for constructing a menorah, playing dreidel, baking cheese *knishes* (ken-ISH-is), and many other fun things. These various activities teach us about Jewish history and culture.

RECIPES

No matter where you find a group of Jewish people, you will most certainly find lots of good food to eat. We want to share some Jewish food with you.

Have you ever had a bagel with lox and cream cheese? Did you know that bagels, pickled herring, pastrami, corned beef, lox, latkes (potato pancakes), chicken soup with matzo balls, rye bread, and pumpernickel bread all come from the Jewish culture?

Jewish recipes have many different flavors. You can't just taste something and know it is a Jewish food. This is because when Jews left their homeland and spread around the world, they picked up different styles of cooking.

There is another important thing we want you to know about. Some Jewish people keep kosher. When people keep kosher, they follow strict rules about preparing and eating all kinds of foods. Kosher foods have a symbol that shows they have been approved by a special rabbi.

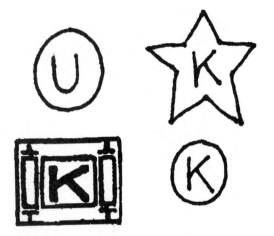

The reason why observant Jews keep kosher is because it is one way to make everyday things into something holy.

Here are some facts about keeping kosher. Dairy (milk) products are never eaten at the same time as meat. For example, cheeseburgers aren't kosher because cheese and meat aren't supposed to be served together. Even Jews who don't keep kosher often don't eat pork or shellfish. For any other meat to be kosher, certain rules have to be followed when it is raised and butchered.

Some foods are *pareve* (par-uh-vuh). This means they are neither meat nor dairy. Fruits, vegetables, grains, fish, and anything that does not contain dairy products or meat products are all pareve.

You can buy kosher food in most supermarkets. There are a number of symbols which indicate if store-bought foods are kosher. Did you know that Reeses Peanut Butter Cups are kosher? So are Hershey's chocolate bars, Grape Nuts, Coca-Cola, plain Fritos, and many more. When you want to buy something kosher, just look for the special symbols on the package. For a kosher friend, you might want to buy some snacks and serve them right out of the sack.

As you can see, there is a lot to learn about keeping kosher. If you really want to know what to serve for a friend who eats kosher, talk your food plans over with your friend ahead of time.

Now we want to share some fun food facts and yummy recipes with you.

Chicken Soup

Chicken soup is known as the "cure-all" Jewish medicine. Maybe your mother has given you chicken soup when you were sick in bed. Have you ever noticed how it always seemed to help? Chicken soup is a great gift to give to a sick friend.

1 whole chicken cut up
  (fryer or roaster)
3 medium size carrots
2 stalks of celery
1 onion
  water (to cover the chicken)
  salt to taste
  pepper to taste

Directions:
1. Wash hands.
2. Find a large pot.
3. Get a fairly big roaster or fryer chicken, unwrap and wash it. Put it in the pot with water, salt, and the vegetables. Add water if the chicken isn't covered.
4. Bring the water to a boil, and then lower the heat.

5. Put a lid over it and cook for about two hours or until the food gets tender.

6. Scoop out the gooey goop that rises to the top every now and then.

7. Take out the chicken and throw away the vegetables that have lost their flavor.

8. Put the soup in the refrigerator and, when it is cold, skim off the fat from the chicken broth. Remove chicken.

9. Save the chicken meat to eat at another dinner.

10. Some people will add new vegetables to the broth and cook until they are soft. This recipe makes about 6 to 8 servings.

Nana's Matzo Balls

    4 eggs
    1 cup matzo meal
  ½ cup water
  ⅓ cup melted margarine
  ½ tsp. salt
    1 tsp. parsley flakes
      dash of pepper

Directions:

1. Wash your hands.

2. Mix eggs and water.

3. Add matzo meal, salt, and parsley flakes and stir. Add melted margarine and continue stirring.

4. Chill the mixture at least two hours in the refrigerator.

5. Wet your hands and roll the mixture into balls a little smaller than a golf ball.

6. Put the balls in boiling salted water or chicken broth. Boil for ½ hour.

7. Use a slotted spoon to get the matzo balls out of the boiling water.

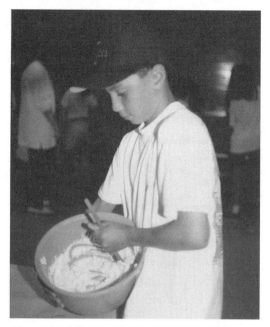

Mixing dough for matzo balls

8. Add the matzo balls to hot chicken soup. This recipe makes about 12 matzo balls.

Sephardic Charoset

This Jewish recipe, like many others, can be made many different ways. It is eaten at Passover with matzo. Jewish Americans, as well as many other Jews around the world, eat this to remind them of the horrible time they had working with mortar for the Egyptians. *Sephardic Charoset* (sif-far-DIK Kha-ro-SIT) is crumbly and tastes sweet. It is very good. Sometimes it tastes like apple pie even though it looks like brown paste.

  ½ cup chopped pitted dates
  ½ cup dried apricots
   2 apples—peeled, cored and chopped
  ½ cup chopped walnuts
   2 tbsp. red grape juice

pinch of cinnamon
pinch of sugar

Directions:
1. Wash your hands.
2. Cut up the pitted dates and the apricots.
3. Put all the ingredients—except the walnuts, cinnamon, and sugar—into the pot or the crock pot and cover it with water.
4. Cook on top of a stove, in a microwave, or in a crock pot until all the fruit is soft and thick.
5. Mash up the fruit with a fork or potato masher.
6. Add the walnuts to the mixture when you are ready to serve it.
7. Add sugar and cinnamon if it needs it.

Aunt Birdie's Noodle Kugel

Almost everybody has had spaghetti, but there are other ways to use noodles. The Jewish people have a great use for pasta. They make a dish called Noodle *Kugel* (COO-gul). We're glad that recipes are still passed down from generation to generation so that they are not lost. This recipe tastes sweet and delicious! We would recommend it to everyone.

 8 oz. of noodles (wide noodles are better)
 3 eggs, beaten
 1 cup of cottage cheese
 1 cup orange yogurt or sour cream
 ⅔ cup milk
 ½ cup sugar
 4 tbsp. melted margarine
1½ tsp. vanilla
 ½ cup raisins or crushed pineapple
1½ tsp. of cinnamon
1–2 tsp. of sugar

Directions:
1. Wash your hands.
2. Cook the noodles in a pot on the stove following the directions on the package.
3. When the noodles are done, drain off the water in the sink.

4. Put all the other ingredients into a large bowl and mix them together with a spoon.
5. Add the noodles.
6. Put everything into a greased 9" x 13" inch pan.
7. Sprinkle top with cinnamon and sugar.
8. Cook at 350 degrees for 1 hour.
This recipe serves 12 people.

Honey Cake

Have you ever had sweet bread? Honey cake is almost like a Jewish sweet bread. Jews all around the world eat honey cake on Rosh Hashana because it reminds them to have a sweet year. If you want to learn more about Rosh Hashana, turn to the Holidays chapter.

½ cup oil
½ tsp. salt
1 cup sugar
½ tsp. cinnamon
4 eggs, beaten
1 cup orange juice
1 cup honey
   grated rind of 1 orange
2½ cup flour
½ cup chopped walnuts
½ cup chopped raisins
1 tsp. allspice
½ tsp. baking soda*
3 tsp. baking powder*
(* use half this amount at elevations above 5,000 feet)

Directions:
1. Wash your hands.
2. Preheat oven to 350 degrees.
3. Mix the oil and the sugar together.

4. Add the eggs one at a time and make sure the mixture is fluffy.
5. Little by little, add the honey.
6. In a different bowl, mix the flour, baking soda, baking powder, allspice, cinnamon, and grated orange rind. (Grate it lightly so you don't get any of the bitter white part.)
7. Add half of flour mixture and ½ cup of orange juice in a large bowl. Mix it all together.
8. Add the rest of the flour and orange juice and mix again.
9. Add the walnuts and the raisins and mix really well.
10. Pour half the batter into one greased 5" x 9"pan and the other half into another greased 5" x 9" pan.
11. Put the pan in the oven right away or the raisins might sink to the bottom.
12. Bake for 45 minutes or until the top springs back when you barely touch it.

Sukkot Fruit Salad

Sukkot means "celebrating harvest." We enjoy the fruits from the harvest, and what better way to celebrate this than to eat a sweet, healthy, and filling fruit salad! We really liked this fruit salad. We especially like the fact that you can put any fruit you want in it!

Here are some examples of the different fruits you can use:
   apples
   oranges
   bananas
   pineapples
   melons

Be sure to have:
honey (for flavor)
lemon juice (so fruit won't turn
    brown)

Directions:
1. Wash your hands.
2. Wash all the fruit (except for the pineapples and bananas, of course!).
3. Remove the seeds and cores from all the fruit.
4. Peel any fruit that needs to be peeled.
5. Cut the fruit into bite-size pieces and put them into a big bowl.
6. Sprinkle a little bit of lemon juice over the fruit.
7. Add one big spoonful or more of honey and mix it all up.

Two authors make Sukkot fruit salad

Hamantashen

It may sound silly, but hamanta[...]
ies look like little hats with three corners, and in fact that's exactly what they're supposed to look like. These delicious cookies symbolize Haman's hat. They are served on Purim. If you want to know more about Haman and Purim, look at the Holidays chapter. If you want to try a delicious cookie, taste a hamantashen. The fillings are excellent!

2 cups flour
½ cup sugar
2 eggs
½ cup margarine
1 tsp. baking powder*
½ tsp. vanilla
½ tsp. grated orange rind
1 tsp. orange juice
(* use only ½ teaspoon of baking powder in high altitude)
Fillings (these can all be bought in cans):
    jams
    apples
    prune butter
    poppy seeds
    almond filling

Directions:
1. Wash hands.
2. Mix all ingredients (except filling) and beat together. If the dough is too wet, add a little more flour. If the dough is too floury, add a little more juice. Shape into a round dough ball.
3. Sprinkle some flour on the table.
4. Roll out the dough so that it is about as thick as a pencil.

Authors make potato latkes

5. Use a round cookie cutter to cut out circles the size of a baseball.

6. Put a spoonful of filling in the center of the circle.

7. Since you need to shape it into a triangle, lift the right and left side up and pinch them to make a corner.

8. Lift the bottom side and pinch the ends to make it look like a triangle or like Haman's hat.

9. Place cookies on a greased cookie sheet about one inch from each other.

10. Bake at 350 degrees for 20 minutes. This recipe makes about 4 dozen hamantashen cookies.

Potato Latkes

Why are latkes eaten on Hanukkah? Potato latkes are cooked in oil. The reason some Jews eat latkes on Hanukkah is because it reminds them of the miracle of the oil lasting eight days on the menorah Hanukiyah. You can read more about this in the "Holidays" chapter. Here is a recipe we think you will like.

    5   medium potatoes
    ¼   onion
    2   eggs
    2   tbsp. flour
    ½   tsp. salt
        oil

Directions:
1. Remember to get help from an adult!
2. Wash your hands.

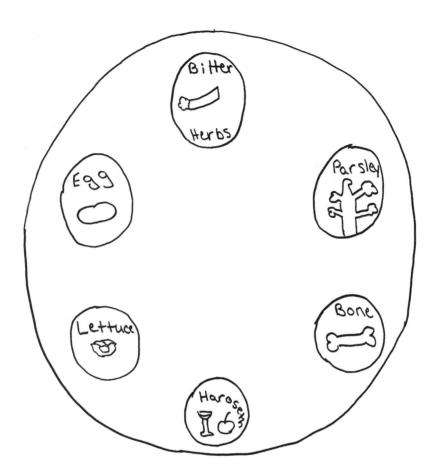

3. Grate the potatoes and squeeze out the juice. Put in a bowl. Grate the onion or cut it up and add to potato.

4. Add the egg, flour, and salt.

5. Mix it all together.

6. Heat up the oil, butter, or shortening.

7. Put the batter in the hot oil, making a pancake shape about three inches wide.

8. Fry the latke until it is brown, then flip it and do the same thing to the other side. Do this with all the latkes.

9. Place the latkes on a paper towel until the extra oil drips off.

10. Eat them with applesauce or sour cream. Yummy!

DAIRY RECIPES

In the Jewish culture there are many delicious dairy recipes. The reason for this is that the holiday of Shavuot is a traditional time to eat dairy because the Jews didn't eat meat until they got the Torah and learned the kosher laws. Some of our favorite recipes were the creamy *blintzes* (BLIN-zis) and the great cheese knishes that have been around America for centuries.

Cheese Blintzes

Cheese blintzes are sort of like a cheese burrito. Make plenty because they disappear amazingly fast. We're sure your friends will like them.

- 2 cups creamed cottage cheese or farmer's cheese
- 2 tbsp. sour cream
- 1 egg yolk
- 1½ tbsp. sugar
- ¼ tsp. salt
- ½ tsp. vanilla (optional)
- ½ pkg. prepared crepes

Directions:

1. Buy some crepes at the market.
2. Wash your hands.
3. Mix everything together except the crepes to make the creamy filling.
4. Put about 2 tablespoons of filling in the middle of each prepared crepe.
5. Roll up the crepes.
6. Fry them in margarine until they are golden brown.
7. Serve with berries, applesauce, sour cream, powdered sugar, honey, or another topping of your choice.
8. Enjoy!

Cheese Knishes

Cheese knishes are just cheese wrapped in a yummy crust. You can put different things besides cheese in a knish. Try meat or potatoes sometime!

- 1 pkg. of puff pastry sheets
- 1 8 oz. container of ricotta cheese
- 1 8 oz. pkg. farmer's cheese
- 2 egg yolks
- 1 tsp. of salt
  water

The authors make holiday crafts

Directions:
1. Wash your hands.
2. Get a medium-size bowl.
3. Mix all the cheeses together.
4. Add the egg yolks and the salt.
5. Take the puff pastry out of the box and unroll it.
6. Stretch or roll it out to be a little longer than a sheet of notebook paper. Cut it about halfway through in about 12 pieces.
7. Spread the cheese filling in a long row on the pastry puff. Roll it up like a jellyroll and then put it on a greased cookie sheet.
8. Bake it in the oven at 400 degrees for 15–20 minutes or until it takes on a golden brown color.
9. Finish making cuts.

CRAFTS

In this section, we teach you how to make fun holiday crafts. We hope you'll enjoy them just as much as we did, maybe even more! There are many fun projects you can do for each holiday, such as making a mask, a candle, and a menorah.

Passover Seder Plate

In our workshop, we made our own plates for a Seder ceremony. Each plate had five or six sections for the symbols important to Passover. Kids made all kinds of plates that were colorful and different. It was easy to do and fun, too.

Materials:
1 white plastic plate
permanent markers (assorted colors)

Directions:
1. Divide the plate into five or six sections with a marker.
2. Label the sections with these words: lamb bone, egg, parsley, maror (a bitter herb), and charoset. Each of these items is symbolic to the Seder.
3. Draw pictures of these things in the proper section.
4. Color the plate as you wish.

Sukkah

Many Jewish people build a sukkah in their backyard for the purpose of eating and sometimes sleeping in it during the holiday of Sukkot, which celebrates the harvest. It is a temporary hut. Many people believe that the American holiday of Thanksgiving came from the Pilgrims reading about Sukkot in their Bibles. Some sukkahs are like a small shed covered with leaves and branches. There are many different ways to make a sukkah.

Materials:
shovel
4 wooden posts
7 boards each 2" x 4" x 8'
6 boards each 1" x 1" x 6'
hammer
nails
heavy cloth (canvas, denim, or waterproof material), about 16 yards square
tacks
tree branches or bamboo poles

Directions:
1. Before your begin, think about how you would build a fort. First, get the four posts and stand them up about 6 feet apart from each other. You may need to dig holes to get the wood to stand up.
2. Nail some wood around the top of each of the four posts.
3. Nail some more wood around three sides. Leave one side open for the entrance.
4. Lay the cloth over the sides and tack it to the wood.
5. Lay some tree branches across the top for a roof. Don't cover it all up, you want to see the sky inside your sukkah.
6. Decorate the sukkah with fruits to remind you of the harvest holiday. Hang them on strings from the branches.

Another way to build a model of a sukkah in your class is to use a refrigerator box. Paint the inside to look like night and hang or glue stars to the top. Then you can hang the fruits from the sides of the box.

Menorah

A menorah is a candleholder used during Hanukkah. You can make menorahs any way you want as long as you make nine holes in it for candles. One candle has to be higher than all the others. That one is called the *Shamash* (SHAH-mash) candle, or service candle. If you want your menorah to be kosher, you will need the eight candles to all be the same height. You can read more about Hanukkah in the Holidays chapter.

Materials:
modeling compound or self-hardening clay
glitter or sequins
tempura paint
paint brushes
glue
candles, special Hanukkah candles (can be bought at the local supermarket)

Menorahs made by the authors

Directions:

1. Think of a shape you'd like and then form the modeling clay that way.

2. Make holes in the shape to put your candles into.

3. Decorate it with paint, glitter, and sequins. You can also use markers after it dries. It takes about 24 hours to dry, depending on what kind of clay you use.

Mishloach Manot

On Purim, Jewish people give baskets called *Mishloach Manot* (mish-la-KA ma-note). In Hebrew, this means "Gifts of Kindness." These baskets are full of sweets and include the three-cornered hamantashen cookies that are made for the Purim holiday. At least two types of sweets are in each basket. These baskets are given to family and friends. Maybe you could make these baskets and spread a little kindness, too.

Materials:
23 or 24 popsicle sticks
glue
black felt-tipped pen
assortment of fruits (raisins, grapes, apples, oranges)
hamantashen
candies

Directions:

1. Make the bottom by gluing 5 popsicle sticks across two sticks, leaving about 1 centimeter between the five sticks. The two long sticks are as far apart as possible.

2. Next, you need four sides. Cut four sticks in half. Glue three whole sticks to two of the half sticks as far apart as possible.

3. Then glue the four sides to the bottom.

4. Put hamantashen, assorted fruits and candies inside. Give to friends.

Purim Mask

If you like to dress up for Halloween, you'll like this Jewish holiday. You get to wear masks and go to carnivals. We made masks in our workshop this summer. Some masks covered only the eyes and others covered the whole face.

Materials:
modeling compound
clay tools
paint (acrylic or tempura)
wax paper
glitter, sequins, and feathers for decorating
brushes

Making a Purim mask

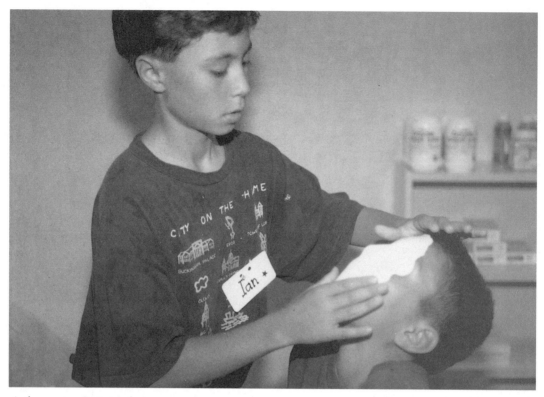

Authors create a Purim mask

glue
rolling pin
newspaper

Directions:
1. Roll the clay around in your hand, then flatten it with your hands or a rolling pin on a piece of wax paper.
2. Put the clay on your face or a friend's face and shape it, making openings for the nose, eyes, and mouth. Keep it there for around three minutes so it holds its shape. You can also make a flat mask.
3. Put the clay mask on wax paper. Use newspaper if you need to prop it up on something.
4. Now paint and let dry. You can decorate it if you want. It takes about 24 hours for the mask to dry. Once your mask is finished, you'll need some old clothes for a costume. Then you'll be ready for Purim!

GAMES

The Jews were very creative people when it came to games, and in this section we have a variety of fun Jewish games to share with you. Some of the games are Jewish, some are Israeli, and some were used by teachers to help kids learn. Many of these games are played at family celebrations, summer camps, and religious schools all across America. We had fun playing them and we hope you will, too.

Dreidel

Children play with *dreidels* at Hanukkah. Jews started using a dreidel a long time ago during the Greek rule over Israel, when they were not allowed to study the Torah in public. They had a lookout man who watched for the enemy soldiers. When a soldier came, the lookout man would yell to the Jews that someone was coming and the Jews would hide their Torah and get out their dreidels. This made it look like they were just playing a harmless game. When the enemies left, the Jewish people could take out their Torahs again and continue studying!

The dreidel has four sides. Each side has a Hebrew letter that stands for something special. Most of all it stands for this important message: "A great miracle happened there." Today the dreidel is a game most Jews play on Hanukkah.

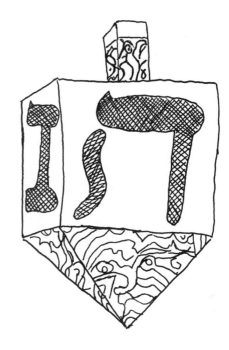

A student's drawing of a dreidel

Directions:

1. Each player puts in one token to start a pot. Tokens can be peanuts, gelt (a chocolate coin wrapped in foil), or anything you might want.
2. The first person spins the dreidel.
3. When the dreidel stops, the person reads the letter that shows.
4. If you get:

 GIMMEL (GREAT)—you get everything from the pot

 NUN (MIRACLE)—you get nothing from the pot

 HEY (HAPPENED)—you get to keep half the pot

 SHIN (THERE)—you must put one token in the pot

5. Then the next person does the same thing. You play until the pot is gone. After everyone has a turn, put in another token and start again.

Gaga

One game we played in our summer workshop is a Jewish game called *Gaga*. Gaga is a game that was invented in Israel. Gaga is fun and is similar to the game we know as dodge ball. You try to hit another person in the circle between the feet and the knees with the ball. Then they are out. Remember not to throw the ball too hard. This is fun to play with your friends outdoors.

What you need:

gym ball or four-square ball (Get one that is not too hard.)

six or more players

a large open area in which to play

Directions:

Form a circle. The size of the circle will depend on the number of players you have. You do not want the circle to be too big or it will be harder for you to get people out of the game. Next, the person who has the ball bounces it three times and then says "Gaga" and throws the ball at a person. If you hit a person below the knees, then they are out. If the person catches the ball, then it is that person's turn to throw the ball. You keep on taking turns until everybody is out except for one person. The last person remaining is the winner. This game can either be played inside or outside. We hope that all teachers are able to teach this game to their students because we had fun learning and playing it.

Chamesh Avanim

One of the most popular Jewish games is called *Chamesh Avanim* (hah-MEHSH EH-vehnim). It means "Five Stones." This game is very similar to the American game of jacks. You need five stones to play. The stones can be bought at the store or just find some outside. The way you play this game is to first throw your five stones on the ground. After that, you pick up one stone and throw it up in the air. While it is in the air, you have to try to pick up one of the other stones off the floor or ground, then catch the falling stone before it hits the ground. If you are successful in picking up the stone the first time, you get to try again, but this time you must pick up two stones. You keep on doing this until all four stones are picked up. If you miss the first time, then it is the next person's turn. You go around in a circle taking turns.

When we played this game in our summer workshop, we found that at times it was frustrating, but also challenging. When you catch the first stone it is exciting, like in jacks. We discovered that in some ways we liked this game more. For one thing, the stones cannot be broken like jacks can be, but in jacks you have more stages. You can make Chamehs Avanim a more challenging game by throwing two stones at the same time you pick up a third.

We hope you will try to make or cook or play all these things and that you will enjoy them and pass them along to all of your friends.

OUR VISION FOR A BETTER TOMORROW

Just imagine what could be done if all of the people of the world would just put their differences behind them and worked together for one day. As we wrote this book, we worked together to celebrate the Jewish heritage. We found out we should not be afraid of people or things that are different.

Each one of us needs to be proud of who we are. We can help make peace by sharing what we believe and by being proud of our cultures. Instead of arguing, fighting, or name-calling, we can all learn to listen to the feelings of others. We can keep what is special to us while working to get along with everyone in the world.

Here are some thoughts that the Jewish writers in the workshop want to share with you:

- We are glad to live in America where people are free to practice their beliefs.
- We want kids to make the world a better place. Do something good in your life and be proud of it.
- We love being Jewish and wouldn't want to change religions even if we could.
- We are all humans and breathe the same air even though our traditions and beliefs are a little different.
- We are proud of our history and roots. No one can take that from us.
- One way to improve the world is to learn about our own heritage and other peoples' heritages, too.
- To me, being Jewish is lighting the candles on Sabbath night. It warms my soul.
- I hope that maybe someday we can live in a world filled with harmony.

❖ Keep on living. No matter what, don't give up!

❖ I love being Jewish!

❖ One thing I feel that is unique about me is that I try to enjoy everything I do because it makes it easier.

❖ The world can change. The world will change. Let it start with me.

❖ One of my parents is Jewish and the other is Christian.

❖ To me, being Jewish means being close to my family and getting a strong education.

❖ Learning about my heritage is a special gift given to me by my parents that I can share with other people.

❖ By writing this book, I have learned how we all need to be more respectful of everyone we know and meet.

❖ Each one of us is different and special for being who we are. Always be proud of who you are.

❖ There is something special about every human being. I hope we can all work together. Keep that in mind as you're reading this book.

Here are some of the things that the non-Jewish writers learned while they were writing this book:

❖ It is always important to respect all heritages. By respecting others, we earn respect.

❖ I really liked learning about Jewish stuff.

❖ I don't like to fight with or tease other people because it makes them feel bad.

❖ I am proud to be Hispanic. I've learned that not all Jewish people are the same and that our cultures are a lot alike. We think family, religion, education, and being your best are important!

❖ When I first came to the workshop, I was a little jealous because I wanted to be Jewish. Now I am glad to be me because I'm unique.

❖ Even though I'm not Jewish, I respect the Jewish heritage. They have wonderful holidays and food. I hope you respect the Jewish heritage, too.

❖ I'm African American and I never make fun of others.

❖ We think that if everyone would respect others and themselves, the world would be a better place.

❖ We may celebrate different things, but we are all Americans.

❖ I'm special because I'm Catholic and Mexican American. I have learned that even though people are different from me, we should all get along.

❖ We have realized how special it is for all of us to be different. It gives us an opportunity to learn something new. It keeps life interesting.

❖ When I came here, I didn't know anything about Jewish people, but now I know a lot. I hope others can learn even more.

❖ I'm Irish and had fun learning about the Jewish heritage. I hope you have fun reading about it, too.

All of us want to thank you for reading our book. We all wrote this book and hope that you will learn from it. We hope that everyone can learn to work together and treat each other the way that they would like people to treat them. We believe that if we try hard to be proud of ourselves and treat other people with respect, the world really can be a better place.

A student's drawing showing the 12 tribes of Israel

WESTRIDGE YOUNG WRITERS
WORKSHOP PARTICIPANTS

STUDENT AUTHORS

Rebecca D. Abrams
Billiemarie Alire
Alexandra B. Allen
Jacob Allen
Jill Hutton Altenhofer
Cameron I. Anderson
Tyler Anstett
Karlo A. Armijo
Steve Armijo Jr.
Jennifer Barnes
Devra M. Barter
Joel Belk
Monica Beston
Jesse Martin Biggs
Aron Bignell
Anna Blumenthal

Aaron Scott Brachfeld
Ian Chase Cadorna
Jonathan Carter
Laura J. Chavez
Stephanie L. Chavez
Nathan Christensen
Shelley E. Cooper
Adam C. Dial
Adam Dillman
Brittany Dooley
Ryan Lynn Dreher
Kevin Everson
Chaya Feder
Shea Feder
Shira M. Feder
Amy D. Fleischman
Amanda Fraley
Garen Fraley

Student authors

Ashley B. Goldstein

Travis M. Goldstein

Daniel Gorton

Jenna D. Gregg

Aaron Hershel Guth

Adam Elan Guth

Rachel Handler

Samuel Handler

Ben Robert Herodes

Jasmin S. Hill

Amy E. Hofmockel

Ursula J. Honigman

Andrea M. Hughes

Linda Irwin

Alyssa Kapnik

Ben Ira Kapnik

Rosie Katz Mount

Sarah Lynn Katz Mount

Maggie M. Kelly

Callie B. Kendrick

Elihv Nathaniel Kenny

Alexis Cummins LeCoq

Aaron Levin

Heather Levin

Beverly R. Levy

Emily C. Lienemann

Melissa R. Loeb

Levi Mark

Jose A. Martinez III

Julio R. Martinez

Nathan Martinez

Jonathan Mathews

Erin May

David Meyer

Erin Miller

Erika Moklestad

Chrissi Moorman

Michal Mor

Eric Muller

Brian J. Noble

Eric Noble

Amy O'Connell

Beth O'Connell

Daniel Higgins Packard

Jacob Pettit

Joey Pettit

Josh Pettit

Shawn M.P. Phelan

David M. Poppleton

Carrie Preziosi

More student authors

Deborah Rhodes
Lauren Ritchie
Joseph H. Romeo
Max J. Rommerdahl
Ari Rosenberg
Alexi Rothschild
Zachary K. Rothschild
David C. Shangraw
Stephanie Soos
Amanda J. Stowe
Jacki M. Thompson
Daniela Uslan
Rachel J. Uslan
Lauren Varner
Elke N. Webb
Matthew D. Zepelin

TEACHER PARTICIPANTS

Annette M. Acevedo-Martinez
Pamela A. Allen
Gail Bell
Nancy Schenk Blumenthal

Tammi Brown
Donna Burris
Roxanne M. Carlson
Susan M. Chichester
Evelyn Cohen
Rebecca C. Compton
Judith H. Cozzens, Director
Kim Goldman
Rosalie Goldman
Karen Guth
Sally Hofmockel
Jan Hutton
Laurie Juran
Robbin R. Kitashima
Karyn Levin
Deborah Levy
Melissa R. Lobach
Julie B. Naughton
Stafie S. Parker
Adrean M. Pepper
Mary Ann Garcia Pettit
Lorena E. Poppleton
Carol Preziosi
Patricia Rhodes

Teacher participants

High school mentors

Roberta "Cookie" Rosenbaum
Susan I. Samuel
Suzi Scher
Cherie Karo Schwartz
Saundra Shidler
Jonathon Simon
Shannon Spense
James G. Yabrove

MENTORS

Daniel Isaac Ariel
Samantha Carter
Jeremy N. Dillman
Lori Earl
Shari A. Epstein
Andrea Samuel Lipstein
Emily M. Phelan
Dorothy Poppleton
Arianne Stein
Marshall J. Zelinger

OTHER PARTICIPANTS

Laurie Blumberg, Steering Committee
Marge Copley, Steering Committee
Wendy Handler, Steering Committee

Jari Kolterman, Editor
Elaine Kusulas, Steering Committee
Mathew Kwartin, Steering Committee
Lev and Miriam Lawrence, Steering
   Committee
Ruth Lipstein, Steering Committee
Suzi Malman, Steering Committee
MaryJo Regier, Photographer
Rose Roy, Administrative Assistant
Anita Wenner, Steering Committee

OTHER PEOPLE WHO DONATED THEIR TIME

Joan Arpin
Kathy Barnes
Sarah Beck
Stan Beiner
Susan Berson
Jay and Rudy Boscoe
Sheila Brachfeld
Sandie Brown
Stephanie DePorte
Avlana Eisenberg
Leah Elias
Susie Feder
Alissa Forrest
Cantor Martin Goldstein
Gail Goodman
Ellen Hochberg
Daisy Herodes
Kathy Herodes
May Hill
Ron Horn
Barb Kelly
Gail Kendrick
Bonnie Kossoff
Cindy LeCoq

Karen Loeb
Rabbi Meir Mark
Sherri May
Lynn Meyer
Jeanne Miller
Debbie Murphy
Bing Peng
Dana Piazza
Rabbi James Ponet
Kathryn Prince
Iris Rave
Barb Ritchie
Rabbi Brent Rosen
Silvia Rosenberg
Terry Ryan
Bernie Sayonne
Cherie Karo Schwartz
Janet Shangraw
Les Shapiro
Amy Sherman
Mark Skeens
Lisa Skidmore
Felix Sparks
Dee Smith
Alysa Stanton
Jerice Stowe
Rachal Tarrasch
Sue K. Varner
Tom Vidas
Glory Weisburg
Judy Zepelin

Temples, synagogues, and other organizations that assisted with presentations, merchandise, or money include the following:

Byers Children's Library
Central Agency for Jewish Education

Denver Public Library
Hebrew Alliance
Herzl Day School
Mizel Museum of Judaica, Denver
National Federation of Temple Youth
Slifka Center at Yale University
Temple Emanuel
Temple Sinai
Westridge Elementary P.T.A.
Westridge Elementary Staff

Thanks also to all these business establishments that donated their resources:

Albertson's
American Traditions
Applebees
Blimpies
Boston Market
Chicago City Deli
Denny's
Denver Salad Company
Grocery Warehouse
Jackson's Hole Sports Grill
King Soopers
Le Peep's
McDonald's
Monaco Inn
Old Chicago
The Olive Garden
Ramon's Mexican Restaurant
Safeway
Tony Roma's Restaurant

CALENDAR

Jewish Americans celebrate many of the same holidays other Americans do, but they also enjoy many holidays, celebrations, and festivals that are unique to Judaism. This calendar includes a list of some important dates in the Jewish calendar, as well as festivals and special events throughout the year.

Most Jews celebrate the Sabbath (called *Shabbat* or *Shabbos*) which lasts from sundown on Friday until sundown on Saturday throughout the year. The Sabbath is considered one of the holiest of the Jewish holidays. Each Sabbath is a time of rest and renewal. For Jews, the Sabbath is a time for families to be together, to think about the past week, and for everyone to give thanks to G-d.

Remember, Jewish holidays follow the lunar calendar, not the common civil calendar you're probably used to. This means that holidays fall on different dates every year. For this reason, we've given you the dates of holidays through 1998. We've begun our calendar with September, since the Jewish New Year falls during that month. For more information on holidays, read the "Holidays and Festivals" chapter in this book.

September

Jewish Renaissance Fair, Sept. 1 in 1996 (New Jersey)—Held annually on the Sunday of Labor Day weekend, the fair features theater, music, and comedy all day long. Great food, carnival games, and other fun activities are also presented. Sponsored by the Rabbinical College of America, 226 Sussex Avenue, P.O. Box 1996, Morristown, NJ 07960; (201) 267-9404.

Rosh Hashanah (Jewish New Year), Sept. 14–15 in 1996; Oct. 2–3 in 1997; Sept. 21–22 in 1998 (Worldwide)—This is the

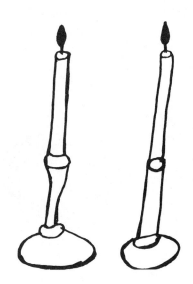

Jewish New Year festival and one of the High Holy Days of the Jewish calendar. During Rosh Hashanah, the *shofar* (ram's horn) is blown during the morning synagogue services. The New Year is the time to reflect on our deeds and thoughts during the past year, and to consider how to make the coming year better for ourselves, our community, and the world.

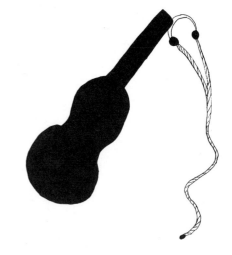

October

Yom Kippur (Day of Atonement), Sept. 23 in 1996; Oct. 11 in 1997; Sept. 30 in 1998 (Worldwide)—This is the most solemn day of the year for Jews. They devote themselves to fasting, prayer, and repentance, and to making themselves ready to begin the year with a clean slate.

Sukkot, Sept. 28–29 in 1996; Oct. 16–17 in 1997; Oct. 5–6 in 1998 (Worldwide)— This festival remembers the period after the Israelites fled Egypt when they lived in huts in the wilderness. Many Jewish people remember this seven-day holiday by building and decorating *sukkahs,* which are huts. Family and friends gather to eat and celebrate in the sukkah throughout the holiday.

Simchat Torah (The Rejoicing of the Torah), Oct. 16–17 in 1996; Oct. 5–6 in 1997; Oct. 23–24 in 1998 (Worldwide)— Observed at the end of Sukkot, Simchat Torah celebrates the completion of the yearly reading of the Torah. There is singing, dancing, and great joy.

November

Jewish Book Month, celebrated during the four weeks before Hanukkah—For more information, contact Jewish community centers, schools, and synagogues in your area.

December

Hanukkah (Festival of Dedication), Dec. 6–13 in 1996; Dec. 24–31 in 1997; Dec.

14-24 in 1998 (Worldwide)—This holiday celebrates the victory of the Maccabees and the rededication of the Second Temple in 165 B.C.E. Jewish communities in cities around the world hold festivals in honor of this occasion. Lighting candles is also an important part of this festival, so Hanukkah is also called the Feast of Lights.

January

Tu B'Shevat (The New Year of the Trees), January–February—Based on an ancient holiday, Tu B'Shevat observes the coming of spring, the renewal of nature, and the importance of the environment. Jewish people celebrate by planting trees, caring for the environment, and gathering for a special meal.

March

National Jewish Music Festival, March–April (U.S.)—The Jewish Music Council encourages the entire nation to celebrate Jewish Music Month (lasting from Purim to Passover) through concerts, lectures, and displays. For more information, write to Jewish Music Festival, 15 East 26th Street, New York, NY 10010.

Purim, Mar. 12 in 1997; Mar. 2 in 1998 (Worldwide)—The merriest of all the Jewish festivals, Purim celebrates the bravery of Queen Esther, a Jew who foiled a plot to destroy the Jews of Persia. During this time, many Jews make Hamantaschen cookies and masks, topping the evening off with a festive meal and a reading of the Book of Esther.

April

Jewish Heritage Week, Apr. 21–28 in 1997 (U.S.)—Celebrated by public and private schools, communities, and organizations across the country. Promotes understanding and greater appreciation for each other's cultures. Sponsored by Jewish Community Relations Council NY, 711 Third Avenue, New York, NY 10017; (212) 983-4800 ext. 142.

Yom Ha' Shoah (Day of Holocaust Remembrance), Apr. 16 (U.S.)—This day commemorates the victims of the Holocaust of World War II. It is a day of remembrance and mourning. For information, contact United States Holocaust Memorial Museum, 100 Raoul Wallenberg Place S.W., Washington, D.C. 20024; (202) 488-0400.

Pesach (Passover), Apr. 17–18 in 1997; Apr. 1–2 in 1998 (Worldwide)—Passover, the oldest Jewish festival, celebrates the deliverance of the Jewish people from Egypt to Israel. Seder meals, filled with special

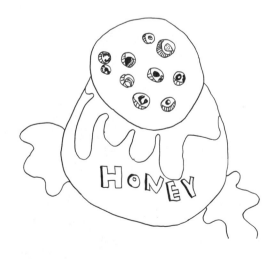

foods and rituals, retell the Biblical story of the Exodus. Often, Jewish families use Passover as a reunion, rejoining family members and friends in this celebration of freedom.

May

International Heritage Fair, late May (California)—This annual fair celebrates the diverse ethnic groups that have made up the history and population of Los Angeles.

Yom ha-Atzama'ut (Israel Independence Day), around May 14 (Israel and U.S.)—This day celebrates the proclamation of independence by the Jews and the establishment of Israel on May 14, 1948. In the U.S., Jews celebrate the holiday by attending concerts, films, parades, Israeli fairs, and

other public events in honor of and thanksgiving for Israel.

Shavuot (Feast of Weeks), May 31–Jun. 1 in 1997; May 21–22 in 1998 (Worldwide)—This holiday symbolizes the reaping of the harvest and the gathering of the Jewish people at Mt. Sinai to accept the Torah, signifying the unity of the Jewish people.

June

Jewish Festival of the Arts, early June (New Jersey)—This festival celebrates Jewish culture. The celebration features Jewish artists, comedians, and dancers. Contact Jewish Festival of the Arts, New Jersey Highway Authority, Garden State Parkway, Woodbridge, New Jersey 07095; (908) 442-9200.

August

Tishah B'Av, August 9—Memorializes the destruction of both the First and Second Temples. This is a day of fasting and prayer.

RESOURCE GUIDE

Here is a list of Jewish-related organizations that might be of help to you. For more information about Jewish groups and activities in your area, contact the Council of Jewish Federations (212) 598-3516. Jewish museums are closed on Saturday and Jewish holidays.

If you can use a computer and get on the internet, the Israel Experience Center has a website at: http://www.teenisrael.org. This site has information about the society, culture, education, and other aspects of Jewish Americans and Israel.

The Center for Judaic Studies, University of Denver, 2199 S. University Blvd., Denver, CO 80208; (303) 871-3020. Provides resource materials for teachers and students. Contact them by mail or phone.

Central Agency for Jewish Education (CAJE) Library and Teacher's Resource Center, 300 S. Dahlia Street, Suite 101, Denver 80222; (303) 321-3191. Call library for schedule of kid-related classes, storytimes, and activities. Provides resource materials, classes for teachers and sutdents, and special-needs programs. There are CAJE's or similar organizations in major U.S. cities. Call the phone numbers listed here to get CAJE's national number.

Council of Jewish Federations (CJF), 730 Broadway, New York, NY 10003-9596; (212) 598-3516. The Council of Jewish Federations is an association of 189 Jewish federations, the central community organization which serves 800 localities, embracing a Jewish population of more than 6 million in the U.S. and Canada. Call CJF to find the council closest to you.

National Museum of American Jewish History, Independence Mall East, 55 N. 5th Street, Philadelphia, PA; (215) 923-3811. Exhibits portray the American Jewish experience from 1654 to the present. Open daily except Saturday. Call for hours and admission.

Judah Magnes Memorial Museum, 2911 Russell Street, Berkeley, CA 94705; (510) 549-6950. Displays Jewish ceremonial art, rare books, textiles, costumes, and collections from Jews around the world. Open Sunday–Thursday 10 a.m.–4 p.m.; closed Friday and Saturday. Call for hours and special exhibits.

Martyrs Memorial and Museum of the Holocaust, 6505 Wilshire Boulevard, Los Angeles, CA 90048; (213) 852-3242. Exhibits and tours include photos, artifacts, art, documents, and videos of the Holocaust. Open Monday–Friday, 9 a.m.–4 p.m.; Sunday, 1 p.m.–5 p.m. Admission is free. Tours must be arranged in advance.

Beit Hashoah–Museum of Tolerance, 9786 W. Pico Boulevard, Los Angeles, CA 90035; (310) 553-9036. Features artifacts, photos, and other exhibits from the Holocaust, World War II, and more recent history. Open Monday–Thursday from 10 a.m. to 4 p.m.; Friday, 10 a.m.–3 p.m.; Sunday, 10:30 a.m. to 5 p.m.; closed Saturday. Admission is $3 for kids ages 3–10; $8 for adults. Call for special events, exhibits.

The Jewish Museum of San Francisco, 121 Steuart Street, San Francisco, CA 94105; (415) 543-8880. Sponsors exhibits, programs for kids, Jewish art, culture, and traditions. Open Sunday–Wednesday, 11 a.m.–6 p.m.; Thursday, 12 p.m.–8 p.m. Closed Friday and Saturday.

Admission is free for kids under age 12. General admission is $3.

Mizel Museum of Judaica, 560 S. Monaco Parkway, Denver, CO 80224; (303) 333-4156. Displays fine art, ritual items, folk art, and contemporary art. Offers guided tours, lectures, exhibits, and programs for kids. Open Tuesday–Friday, 10 a.m–4 p.m.; Sunday, 12 p.m.–4 p.m.; closed Monday and Saturday. Admission is free. Group tours for kids are $1.50. Workshops are also available. Call for more information.

United States Holocaust Memorial Museum, 100 Raoul Wallenberg Place, S.W. Washington, D.C. 20024-2150; (202) 488-0400 ext. 2. The largest and most-visited museum of its kind in the U.S. Exhibits and programs reflect the events of the Holocaust, including artifacts, photos, films, videos, and books. Special exhibits are also available for kids. Children under age 11 must be accompanied by adults. Open daily, 10 a.m.–5:30 p.m. Admission is free.

B'nai B'rith Klutznick National Jewish Museum, 1640 Rhode Island Avenue, N.W. Washington, D.C. 20036; (202) 857-6583. Includes exhibits on Jewish folk and contemporary art, archaeology, historical documents, and Jewish history. Open Sunday–Friday, 10 a.m.–5 p.m. Admission is free.

Kohl Children's Museum, 165 Green Bay Road, Wilmette, Illinois 60091; (312) 256-6056. The museum's model of old

Jerusalem is one of its most popular exhibits. Also includes exhibits on Morocco, pets, and science. Open Tuesday–Saturday, 10 a.m.–4 p.m.; Sunday, 12 p.m.–4 p.m. Closed on Monday. Admission is free.

Morton B. Weiss Museum, K.A.M. Isaiah Israel Congregation, 1100 Hyde Park Boulevard, Chicago, IL 60615; (312) 924-1234. Small museum featuring exhibits on American Jewish history, artifacts of European and Asian Jewish roots, and jewelry. Open daily, 9 a.m.–5 p.m. Closed Saturday. Admission is free.

Spertus Museum, 618 S. Michigan Avenue, Chicago, IL 60605; (312) 922-9012. Includes exhibits of folklore, archaeology, art, and literature. Guided tours for kids are available. Open Monday–Thursday, 10 a.m. to 5 p.m.; Friday, 10 a.m.–3 p.m. Closed Saturday. Admission is $2 for kids; $3.50 for adults.

Jewish Historical Society of Maryland, 15 Lloyd Street, Baltimore, MD 21202; (410) 732-6400. Museum displays photos, manuscripts, ceremonial art, folk art, furniture, and other artifacts from Jewish history. Open Tuesday–Thursday, and Sunday, from 12 p.m. to 4 p.m. Admission is free for kids; $2 for adults.

Harvard University Semitic Museum, 6 Divinity Avenue, Cambridge, MA 02138; (617) 495-4631. Features exhibits on archaeology and Semitic languages and history. Sponsors guided tours, lectures, and special programs. Open Monday–Friday, 10 a.m.–4 p.m.; Sunday, 1 p.m.–4 p.m. Admission is free. Call ahead for information about tours and special exhibits.

American Jewish Historical Society, 2 Thorton Road, Waltham, MA 02154; (617) 891-8110. Collections include portraits and memorabilia of Jewish families from the 1700s to the present. Also includes Yiddish movie posters, ceremonial objects, and early manuscripts. Open Monday–Friday, 9 a.m.–4:30 p.m. Closed Saturday. Admission is free.

Museum of the Southern Jewish Experience, 4915 I-55 N., Suite 204B, Jackson, MS 39206; (601) 362-6357. Museum is located in Utica, but call ahead to set up an appointment. Includes collections of Jewish memorabilia, furniture, jewelry, and historic photos of Jewish life in the Deep South. Has education programs and guided tours for children and adults. Open by appointment any day. Admission is free.

The Jewish Museum, 1109 Fifth Avenue, New York, NY 10128; (212) 423-3200. Contains exhibits featuring Jewish art, history, and culture. Its Judaica collection spans 40 centuries! There is also a children's room with special exhibits, and a crafts room. Open Tuesday, 11 a.m.–9 p.m.; Wednesday–Friday, 11 a.m.–8 p.m.; Sunday, 10 a.m.– 5:45 a.m.; closed Saturday. Admission is free for kids under age 12; adults are $7. Call ahead for special exhibits and children's activities.

Yeshiva University Museum, 2520 Amsterdam Avenue, New York, NY 10033; (212) 960-5390. Exhibits include ceremonial objects in silver and other metals, textiles, rare scrolls and books, photos, fine art, and sculpture. Open Tuesday–Thursday, 10:30 a.m.–5 p.m.; Sunday, 12 p.m.–6 p.m. Closed Saturday. Admission is $2 for kids under age 12; $3 for adults. Call ahead for special exhibits and tours.

Fenster Museum of Jewish Art, 1223 E. 17th Place, Tulsa, OK 74120; (918) 582-3732. Has one of the largest collections of Jewish art in the U.S. Features textiles, costumes, documents, photos, paintings, and other artifacts emphasizing Jewish history, culture, and art. Open Sunday through Thursday, 10 a.m.–4 p.m. Closed Saturday. Admission is free.

Siskin Museum of Religious and Ceremonial Art, One Siskin Plaza, Chattanooga, TN 37403; (423) 634-1700. Includes more than 400 objects of Judaic art in silver, ivory, wood, brass, and pewter. Open Monday–Friday, 8 a.m.–5 p.m. Admission is free.

My Jewish Discovery Place Children's Museum of JCCA, 870 W. Olympic Boulevard, Los Angeles, CA 90035; (213) 857-0036 ext. 9. Collections include hands-on focus on Jewish culture, traditions, history, arts, and religion. Open Tuesday– Thursday, 12:30 p.m.–4 p.m; Sunday, 12:30 p.m.–5 p.m. Admission is $2 for kids ages 3–7; $3 for people age 7 and older.

Dallas Memorial Center for Holocaust Studies, 7900 Northaven, Dallas, TX 75230; (214) 750-4654. Exhibits photographs and artifacts from the Holocaust, and Jewish life in Europe before the Holocaust. Films and guided tours are available.

Open Sunday, 12 p.m.–4 p.m., Monday–Friday, 9:30 a.m.–4:30 p.m. Closed Saturday. Admission is free, but donations are encouraged. Recommended for mature 10-year-olds or older.

Sylvia Plotkin Judaica Museum, 3310 N. 10th Avenue at Osborn Road, Phoenix, AZ 85013; (602) 264-4428. Exhibits Jewish arts from 1600 to the present; original artifacts; pioneer Jews of Arizona, 1850–1920; archaeology of Israel. Guided tours, films, and programs for kids are available. Open Tuesday–Thursday, 10 a.m.–3 p.m.; Sunday, 12 p.m.–3 p.m. Closed Monday and Saturday. Admission is free. Call ahead for tour information.

The Skirball Cultural Center, 2701 N. Sepulveda Boulevard, Los Angeles, CA 90049; (310) 440-4500. Includes a museum, auditorium, discovery center for children, restaurant, and gift store. One of the featured exhibits at the museum is "Visions and Values: Jewish Life from Antiquity to America." The museum also displays contemporary Jewish art, ceremonial art, and historical artifacts. Call ahead for special events and exhibits at the Center.

Institute of Texan Cultures, HemisFair Park, 801 S. Bowie Street, San Antonio, TX 78205; (210) 558-2300. Includes exhibits for kids and adults about 27 ethnic groups in Texas. Daily tours and special exhibits are also available. Admission is $3 for kids ages 3–12; $4 for adults. Open Tuesday–Sunday, 9 a.m.–5 p.m.

PUBLICATIONS

Shofar magazine, 43 Northcote Drive, Melville, NY 11747; (516) 643-4598. Aimed at Jewish children ages 8–14. This 28-page monthly magazine includes stories and articles about Jewish celebrities, holidays, and customs. It also features puzzles, crafts, and other activities.

A Kids Catalog of Israel by Chaya Burstein. Jewish Publication Society, 1988. This is an excellent reference book, full of fun facts, including information about history, geography, songs, dances, holiday celebrations, crafts, and food.

The Jews in America by Milton Meltzer. Jewish Publication Society, 1985. Surveys the history of Jewish immigration to America and presents the lives of Jewish-Americans and their major contributions.

ORGANIZATIONS

B'nai B'rith Youth Organization, Washington, D.C. (202) 857-6633. A youth-run organization established to give its members a strong Jewish identity and leadership experiences, to offer supervised leisure-time activities, and to encourage kids to become responsible members of their family and community.

Coalition for the Advancement of Jewish Education, 261 W. 35th Street, Floor 12A, New York, NY 10001; (212) 268-4210. World's largest organization of Jewish educators in every field.

No matter what culture, everyone needs a family.

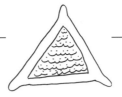

GLOSSARY OF HEBREW AND YIDDISH WORDS

alef-bet (ah-LEF bet)—Hebrew alphabet

Bar Mitzvah (bar MITS-vah)—ritual that celebrates a Jewish boy becoming a man

Bat Mitzvah (baht MITS-vah)—ritual that celebrates a Jewish girl becoming a woman

brit milah (brit MEE-lah)—ritual circumcision

bubeleh (BUB-eh-leh)—little one

bubbeh (BU-beh)—grandmother

Chamesh Avanim (hah-MEHSH EH-vehn-im)—a game, like jacks, played with five stones

chupah (HOO-pa)—wedding canopy

chutzpah (HOOTZ-pah)—nerve or guts

challah (HA-lah)—braided egg bread

dreidel (DRAY-dul)—a top-like toy with a hebrew letter on each side

falafel (fah-LAH-fel)—fried patties of ground chickpeas and spices

hallel (ha-LELL)—psalms of praise sung on certain holidays

hamotzi (ha-MOAT-ze)—a blessing said over the bread

Hanukkah (HAH-nuh-kah)—Festival of Lights celebration that takes place in November or December

Hanukiyah (han-u-KEY-ah)—a candle holder used during Hanukkah

Havdalah (hav-DAH-lah)—a ceremony at the end of shabbat involving wine, spices, and a candle

kaddish (kah-DISH)—a prayer said at daily services and at funerals

kiddush (kid-OOSH)—a blessing said over wine

kohen (KO-hane)—a man who is a direct descendant of Aaron

Kol Nidre (kol NEE-dray)—the first prayer said during Yom Kippur

Kosher (KOH-sher)—allowed by Jewish law

latke (LOT-kah)—potato pancake

L'Chayim (leh-HI-yim)—a toast that means "To life!"

matzo (MAHT-zah)—flat, thin, unleavened (without yeast) bread

mazel tov (MAH-zul tov)—good luck, congratulations

megillah (ma-GEEL-ah)—story

menorah (meh-NOR-ah)—a candelabra of seven branhces described in Exodus

mensch (mensh)—a good-hearted, decent person

mishloach manot (mish-la-KAH ma-NOTE)—gift baskets full of fruits and sweets given on Purim

mishmash (MISH-mash)—mixture, concoction

mitzvah (MITS-vah)—a commandment or good deed, written in the Torah *mitzvot* (mitz-VOTE)—more than one mitzvah; there are 613 mitzvot in the entire Torah

mohel (MO-hell)—man who circumcises the baby boy during the brit milah

nosh (nahsh)—to snack

nudge (nuhj)—to pester

oy vey—an exclamation of surprise or annoyance, similar to "Oh, no!"

pareve (PAR-uh-vuh)—food that does not contain either meat or dairy products

pidyon haben (PID-yon ha-BEN)—redemption ceremony for first-born males

Purim (POO-rem)—spring holiday that celebrates Queen Esther's bravery against the evil Haman

Rosh Hashana (ROSH ha-SHAH-nah)—Jewish New Year, usually falls in the month of September

Sabbath (shah-BAHT)—the day of rest commanded by God in the Ten Commandments. For Jews, the Sabbath lasts from sundown on Friday to sundown on Saturday

schmaltzy (SHMALT-see)—overly sentimental

Seder (SAY-der)—feast eaten on the first night of Passover

Shalom Nekaivah (shah-LOHM nek-AY-vah)—Naming ritual for a baby girl; means "Hello, female"

shamash (SHAH-mash)—highest candle in the menorah

Shavuot (shah-VOO-oht)—holiday celebrating the gift of the Torah, falls seven weeks after Passover

shivah (SHEH-vah)—a period of mourning, lasting three or seven days

Shoah (SHOW-ah)—the Holocaust

shofar (show-FAHR)—a ram's horn that is blown on Rosh Hashana and other holidays in the Jewish years

shul (shool)—synagogue

Simchat Bat (sim-KAHT baht)—celebration of the birth of a baby girl

Simchat Torah (sim-KAT toe-RAH)—holiday that celebrates having finished reading the Torah, follows Sukkot

spiel (shpeel)—story or talk

sukkah (su-KAH)—hut built to celebrate Sukkot

Sukkot (su-KOAT)—fall holiday celebrating of the harvest

tallit (ta-LEET)—prayer shawl

Talmud (TAHL-mood)—Jewish book of law, legend and argument

Tanach (tah-NAH)—Hebrew word for the Bible

tefillin (tah-FILL-in)—two black boxes with prayers inside that are attached to long leather straps; one is worn on the forehead and one is worn on the arm

Tishah b'Av (TEESH-uh BOV)—day of remembrance for the day on which the Holy Temple was destroyed

Torah (TOR-ah)—first five books of the Jewish Bible

tzedakah (tsa-da-KAH)—giving to those who are in need

tzedakahm box (tsa-da-KAHM)—a container for change; when full, the money is donated to charity

yahrzeit (yor-TSIGHT)—candle burned on the anniversary of a person's death

yarmulke (YAH-muhl-kuh)—a skullcap worn by many male Jews

Yom Ha'Atzma'ut (yohm ha-AHTS-mah-oot)—day, usually in April or May, which celebrates the creation of the State of Israel

Yamin Noraim (yah-MEEM no-rah-EEM)—
Jewish High Holidays, the first ten days of
the seventh month on the Jewish calendar.
Begins with Rosh Hashana and ends with
Yom Kippur.

Yom Kippur (yohm kee-POOR)—Day of
Atonement

zayda (ZAY-dah)—grandfather

INDEX

American Origins Series

Each is 48 pages and $12.95 hardcover.
Tracing Our English Roots
Tracing Our German Roots
Tracing Our Irish Roots
Tracing Our Italian Roots
Tracing Our Japanese Roots
Tracing Our Jewish Roots
Tracing Our Polish Roots

Bizarre & Beautiful Series

Each is 48 pages, $14.95 hardcover, $9.95 paperback.
Bizarre & Beautiful Ears
Bizarre & Beautiful Eyes
Bizarre & Beautiful Feelers
Bizarre & Beautiful Noses
Bizarre & Beautiful Tongues

Extremely Weird Series

Each is 32 pages and $5.95 paperback.
Extremely Weird Bats
Extremely Weird Endangered Species
Extremely Weird Fishes
Extremely Weird Frogs
Extremely Weird Reptiles
Extremely Weird Spiders
Extremely Weird Birds
Extremely Weird Insects
Extremely Weird Mammals
Extremely Weird Micro Monsters
Extremely Weird Primates
Extremely Weird Sea Creatures
Extremely Weird Snakes

Kids Go!™ Travel Series

Each is 144 pages and $7.95 paperback.
Kids Go! Atlanta (avail. 1/97)
Kids Go! Cleveland (avail. 2/97)
Kids Go! Denver
Kids Go! Minneapolis/St. Paul
Kids Go! San Francisco
Kids Go! Seattle
Kids Go! Washington, D.C. (avail. 1/97)

Kids Explore Series

Written by kids for kids, each is $9.95 paperback.
Kids Explore America's African American Heritage, 160 pages
Kids Explore America's Hispanic Heritage, 160 pages
Kids Explore America's Japanese American Heritage, 160 pages
Kids Explore America's Jewish Heritage, 160 pages
Kids Explore the Gifts of Children with Special Needs, 128 pages
Kids Explore the Heritage of Western Native Americans, 128 pages

Masters of Motion Series

Each is 48 pages and $6.95 paperback.
How to Drive an Indy Race Car
How to Fly a 747
How to Fly the Space Shuttle

Rainbow Warrior Artists Series

Each is 48 pages, $14.95 hardcover, $9.95 paperback.
Native Artists of Africa
Native Artists of Europe
Native Artists of North America

Rough and Ready Series

Each is 48 pages and $4.95 paperback.

Rough and Ready Cowboys
Rough and Ready Homesteaders
Rough and Ready Loggers
Rough and Ready Outlaws and Lawmen
Rough and Ready Prospectors
Rough and Ready Railroaders

X-ray Vision Series

Each is 48 pages and $6.95 paperback.

Looking Inside the Brain
Looking Inside Cartoon Animation
Looking Inside Caves and Caverns
Looking Inside Sports Aerodynamics
Looking Inside Sunken Treasure
Looking Inside Telescopes and the Night Sky

Other Children's Titles

Habitats: Where the Wild Things Live, 48 pages, $9.95

The Indian Way: Learning to Communicate with Mother Earth, 112 pages, $9.95

Ordering Information

Please check your local bookstore for our books, or call **1-800-888-7504** to order direct and to receive a complete catalog. A shipping charge will be added to your order total.

Send all inquiries to:
John Muir Publications
P.O. Box 613
Santa Fe, NM 87504

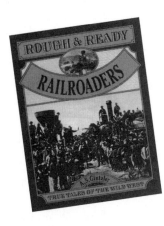